Praise for *Climbing Lessons*

"These poignant stories reveal the universal ways in which parents and parenting can lead us to feel, at once, grateful and disheartened, elated and vulnerable—surprised by joy and by grief. **A remarkable achievement!**"

–John T. Price, author of
Daddy Long Legs: The Natural Education of a Father

Tim Bascom succeeds in creating something **both intensely personal and irresistibly universal**. These are his stories and our stories, celebrating the rewards of parenting done right while confronting the trials that come with learning to reach that summit.

–Tom LaMarr, author of *Geezer Dad*

"*Climbing Lessons* stays close to home, with the **unflinching discoveries** that come from birth, marriage, fatherhood and death, all told with Bascom's **great powers of honesty, humor, and deep sincerity**."

–Thomas Fox Averill, Emeritus Creative Writing Professor at Washburn University, O. Henry Award winner, and author of the novel *Found Documents from the Life of Nell Johnson Doerr*

"Anyone can tell family stories, but few can tell them with such **warm-hearted and arresting details**.... These stories will warm every reader's heart and will set their memory fires burning. **Bascom is an amazing writer**."

–Jim Heynen, author of the story collections
The One-Room Schoolhouse and *Ordinary Sins*

"*Climbing Lessons* is **quiet, wise, and true**."

–Joe Wilkins, author of *Fall Back Down When I Die*
and *The Mountain and the Fathers*

Climbing Lessons

Climbing Lessons

Stories of Fathers, Sons, and the Bond Between

TIM BASCOM

Durham, NC

Climbing Lessons: Stories of Fathers, Sons, and the Bond Between
Tim Bascom
timbascom.wordpress.com
lightmessages.com/tim-bascom
Tim.Bascom@waldorf.edu

Published 2020, by Light Messages
www.lightmessages.com
Durham, NC 27713 USA
SAN: 920-9298

Paperback ISBN: 978-1-61153-344-6
E-book ISBN: 978-1-61153-345-3
Library of Congress Control Number: 2019949545

In honor of Charles Bascom (1931-2015),
who boldly went out in front of us all and showed the way.

Preface

Some movies begin with a disclaimer: "This story is based on real events."

Well, that's the situation here. These stories are based on real events. I've just taken a few liberties so that you won't get bogged down by irrelevant details, such as my father switching to a new job right when you were getting used to the old one.

Hopefully, these pared-down tales have become elemental enough that they will translate over into your own life. I'd like them to be your stories, not just mine. In fact, I initially wrote them in third-person, so that I could step back from who I once was and see that boy—or young man—as a representative male living outside myself.

Basically, I am intrigued by what might be universal in the relationship between sons and fathers, and I am intrigued by what has to change. A toddler is not a teenager, nor a first-time dad. Also, 1970 is remarkably different than 2020. Which means that, while the father and son grow older, always bound by shared experiences, their relationship must evolve.

Here is my attempt to map some of the changes that can be expected. If you want to see more of the terrain, consider reading the stories in tandem with family members or friends, stopping to talk. In my experience such camaraderie is guaranteed to make the hike—the "climb"—more meaningful.

Unimaginable

Once when I was seven or eight, I had a weird realization while gazing into the bathroom mirror contemplating my black bowl of hair and freckled nose. I realized that, long ago, my father might have stood in a bathroom just like me, gazing at his younger self and wondering whether his father had also stood in a bathroom gazing and wondering.

Why did I think this?

Maybe because I had been watching *Gunsmoke* with Dad and started to compare hands, thinking, *How can I, with my small, smooth fingers, be related to this man with such large wrinkled knuckles?*

Later, as he took me up to my attic bedroom to say goodnight, I heard my mother calling after him, "Charles, did I tell you we got a letter from your folks?" And it occurred to me that, if my father was also a son, he was always, in some sense, still a boy. Which meant, of course, that my grandfather was also a boy—though *that* was harder to imagine, what with Grandpa's bushy ears and eyebrows and his tendency to quote Rudyard Kipling:

> If you can fill the unforgiving minute
> With sixty seconds' worth of distance run,
> Yours is the Earth and everything that's in it,
> And—which is more—you'll
> be a Man, my son!

It was hard to picture my steel-grey bewhiskered grandfather as a belt-buckle-height kid with smooth cheeks—to imagine him sitting in a clapboard church in North Dakota listening to his own father who, like God's police officer, proclaimed from the pulpit that the LORD would not abide two things: alcohol or war. My father had once told me that Grandpa was flipped upside down by boys who knew he would not retaliate because his father prohibited fighting. Supposedly, they stuffed manure down his pants' legs. But how was that possible, I wondered? How was it possible that such a calm, unflappable granddad had writhed and kicked until he was on his feet again, flailing, bashing knuckles against a chin, a rib, the side of someone's head? I could imagine myself going berserk, but not that early edition of my surgeon-grandfather. Not Doc K.F., the man with the steadiest hands in town.

Nevertheless, according to legend, my grandpa had once been *that* reactive, that *child-like*. What's more, my own father had once been just as small and out of control. Supposedly, when he was my age, my dad had stolen irises out of the neighbor's yard to give to his mother for Mother's Day; and Grandpa had marched him right back across the lawn to confess this impulsive flower-felony.

Mind-boggling. That's how it seemed. I could not conceive of my father any other way than large and in charge. In fact, I tended to think of him right next to God, conscious that the two had some sort of agreement since he always said the same thing as he tucked me into bed: "God loves you and I love you too."

Unimaginable, this alleged past. And equally mystifying? The future! Out there in front of me lay another absurdity: If my father and grandfather had been boys like me, then someday I too would become a man, might even have a son.

How bizarre to think that there could be an unborn waiting out there—some "other" who might live in an era closer to the one I watched on *Star Trek*, where rocket ships traveled beyond the moon and people carried little flip phones that allowed them to talk wherever they might be. How bizarre that this time-traveling son might look up from his 21st Century pillow thinking as I was thinking while I drifted to sleep: *Once my father was a boy just like me!*

Floating

One summer when our family went to visit Grandma and Grandpa two hours west—in Manhattan, Kansas—we stayed too long. Grandpa kept us there with the way his surgeon hands dissected the sunfish we had caught, slicing behind the gills and ripping the heads away with all the insides dangling: silver intestines and yellow egg sac and rusty liver, to be pinched loose at the anus so the fillets would remain and the rest drop into the bucket with the wormy castoffs. My two brothers and I, like the curious blue-black flies on the rim of the bucket, hovered around the glazed eyeballs and mica-like scales. We loved examining this mucousy stuff as much as drinking our grandma's 7-Up-and-lime-sherbet concoctions, which kept us so late that, when we drove back across the roller coaster hills toward our home two hours away, it was long past nightfall and the sky was a black basin set down over the land.

There was no moon, and I could not see my hands

where I leaned against a back door of the boat-like Impala with my little brother half asleep against me. I watched the beams of the headlights launch off the crested hills, pointing into the moth-filled darkness before swooping down onto the treetops, lighting up reflective signs—Speed Limit 55—and the dotted line that whispered, "Follow me, follow me."

The windows were open because there was no air conditioning. I could feel the warm breeze change as we glided into the valleys—becoming cool and damp, suggestive of streams and oak trees and moist soil with corn growing in it. As we rose again onto the hilltops, the air turned dry and warm, murmuring its message of open prairie, sweet and redolent with the scents of sun-bleached grass and baked cattle droppings.

For some reason, our father slowed as we entered another valley. He pulled the car off the tarmac and eased it down a gravel road.

"Honey?" asked my mother.

"Humor me."

"You have your hospital rounds tomorrow—starting at eight o'clock."

"Just one minute. That's all."

He swung the big sedan into one of the little sidespurs that farmers used to access their fields with tractors, parking it against the barbed wire gate so that the lights pointed out over the two-foot-tall stalks of half-grown corn. Then he turned everything off.

"Daaaad...?" I murmured, because I was only a first or second grader and felt spooked by the sudden black silence.

"Everyone out," he replied. "Just for a minute, that's all. You'll enjoy it, I promise."

"Ah, c'mon," protested my older brother John, speaking loud enough to make my little brother jerk his head upright from where he was slumped against me.

"Only a minute. I'll even let you sit on the hood."

Lured by this unexpected proposal, I eased my door open and stepped into the pit-like darkness, feeling for the ground. I inched forward along the side of the car, keeping my hand on the cold metal until I had reached the front bumper and could climb up.

John was already onto the hood, and I could hear Nat, only three years old, being set down to join him.

The hood popped, and Mom erupted, "This is not a good idea!"

"It'll be fine," said Dad from the other side of the car. "Now everyone be quiet and see what you can see."

Mom sighed, but there was no other sound after that. I just stared up from where I leaned against the cool glass of the windshield. I gave all my attention to the stars, which was a natural thing to do in the moonless dark. The stars were so crisp and glittering that they seemed alive, like pulsing jewels. I felt a kind of visible music throbbing out of them—some sort of celestial, come-on-up-here song that glistened in the wind.

"Open your ears, too," said Dad, and I concentrated hard, picking up the chirping of crickets in the corn and some frogs croaking. A breeze rattled through the corn, and the whole field seemed to rustle in wax paper. The corn was alive, I realized. I could hear it out there in the dark, moving. I could hear it bending and waving its spear-like leaves. I thought I could even hear it stretching toward the stars, lengthening like the antennae of the car, which I had grasped in the dark and lifted.

When we had all eased back into the dark cabin of the car and resumed our trip, Mom leaned over her seatback to say, "You know you boys have a very unusual father." She said it teasingly, as if she had let go of her sharpness. "He made me do things like this back when we were first dating."

Dad chuckled. "So did anybody hear the corn growing?"

"I did!" I called out. And though John said, "Nuh-uh," I didn't bother to argue. I just thought about all that waxpaper crinkling out there in the fields.

Dad brought the Impala up to cruising speed. Then he pushed the gas a bit harder, perhaps because he was trying to make up for lost time, or maybe because he just felt happy. When we peaked the next hill, we were going faster than the speed limit, and as the car pointed heavenward with nothing to see but sky, it was set loose for a moment, released from gravity so that we all floated off our seats.

"Whoa!" shouted my brothers and me as the hood lowered and the car swooped back down the other side of the hill. Although I came down, I could feel my insides rising, lifting like the little float bags in the blue gills.

The car swept into the next valley with headlights glimmering off the ghostly trees and fence posts. I could hear cicadas droning out the windows, giving off their evening incantation. I could see lightning bugs pooled in a pasture, creating a big eddy of incandescence. I wanted to join all this magic, to rise right up with the hills and float away.

"Faster, faster," I called as the car climbed another hillside. And my father seemed to understand, gunning the engine.

Mom protested in a way that suggested she was getting worried. "How much are speeding tickets?" she asked. But Dad was in the right mood now and shot us skyward at more than seventy-miles-an-hour, risking maybe even fifty dollars. When we crowned the hilltop, the car took flight as if leaving a ramp, as if he could pilot us right out into the Milky Way. Only six or seven, I floated up there, looking out the windshield at the clustering stars—the sparkling dipper and the bright belt and all the other stars singing their come-on-up song—and I could feel myself getting closer. This time, I hoped, we would never come down.

Fountain of Youth

To reach it, we had to hike twenty minutes along a little wooded creek that eventually emptied into the Missouri River, which was on the state line just five miles north of our town—Troy, Kansas. During summer, our clothes clung with sweat as we sidestepped spider webs and eased through nettles. We arrived hot and dusty, itchy with mosquito bites. Then my brothers and I dashed ahead, browning trousers as we slid down the muddy bank and jostled for a first turn under the tree-root overhang.

Just to stoop into that damp, mushroomy shade was a relief, but the place felt almost enchanted at times because of a cool breeze exhaled from the ground, emerging along with a burbling spring. The chill air wafted out of a deep hole, feeling like something straight from the fridge. It drifted into the muggy vapor of the ravine, changing the whole mood of the day.

The water from the spring wasn't muddy like

the creek. Rippling, it magnified everything—so that pebbles bulged twice as large, seeming to pulse with their own secret life.

We had to crouch down onto our hands and knees to drink, and we took long turns bowing into the grotto. But our father stayed longest, holding a half push-up with his face nearly submerged. When he backed out, he uttered a big "aaah" as if some much-delayed need had been satisfied. This was the sigh of a man stretching out on a bed after a full day of lifting.

"Years younger," he said, incantation-like, suggesting that he was going to transform before our eyes. And perhaps the water did make him younger because he often turned playful afterward. When we asked him, once, if he would help dig a cave, he surprised us by not hesitating at all: "Sure, let's dig a cave."

Back at the campsite, he helped to pick a rounded knoll and to gather the necessary tools: a shovel, a hatchet, plus a few large serving spoons that might double as hand spades. He cut a circle into a nearby slope, forming a barrel-like entrance. He got right down on his knees, taking turns with us as we reached into the hole and scraped.

The deepening entrance was hardly wider than our dad's torso, so that when he dug, he had to shove dirt between his knees. However, he kept at it, face to the hillside, slowly disappearing, until eventually he had helped us to empty a ball-like interior where we could all squeeze together. Inside there, our sweaty shirts went cool on our backs. The little hollow seemed to exhale the same mysterious mineral breath as the spring—to whisper a hint of some subterranean elixir.

We opened the space a bit further and carved earthen benches. Then we sat and looked at the entrance. In the glimmering light, our father's face was reduced to essentials: a high smudged forehead, a shock of black hair, a well-defined nose. He smiled softly, and for a moment all four of us were silent, savoring our secret hideaway.

Eventually, my older brother spoke, caught up in dream-like thoughts. He pondered, out loud, what it might have been like to come from some magical era when people lived in the ground—an ancient clan with an ancient way to stay young. And as I listened, it seemed to me that Dad had become a large child himself, stooped into our small, shared world.

"If we dig deeper," my little brother asked, "could we find where the spring comes from?"

"Would it be a lake?" I added. "A huge, black lake?"

"Who knows?" Dad whispered. "Who knows?"

Finally, then, we crawled back out into the brilliant sun patches. We blinked and grinned at each other, hearing the jackhammer noises of a woodpecker, the crinkling of leaves under our knees. Emerging from that hole felt like being born back into a new world. It felt like starting everything over.

Climbing Lesson 1

One weekend during the spring of third grade, I went hiking with John and Nat and my dad, continuing further along our favorite creek, at least a mile beyond the spring where we usually stopped. All that was left in the stream bed was a murky dribble—but we came upon a huge sycamore hovering above that trickle. It was a magnificent tree—with a mottled trunk the width of a couch and grand limbs that stretched forty feet to each side. Best of all, the lean of the trunk made it seem like a sort of living ramp. Come on up, it begged.

Since I got there first, I started a cautious attempt to climb, straddling the huge trunk and hitching myself up. However, I lost strength six feet up and had to slide back down.

John, three years older, took his turn, too, trying to tightrope-walk slowly up the incline, but he lost his balance and had to jump down. And when our little brother failed, Dad broke in: "Alright, lads, step aside.

Time for the old man to show you how it's done."

To our surprise, he walked away from the tree instead of towards it. Then he turned and arched backwards, chest extended, arms out as if to say, "Behold!" And he took a galloping start, mounting that impressive incline in five huge steps.

Our father was a big man with a top-heavy torso. His pant cuffs flapped. His keys jangled. But he was a sight to see, so large up there and not stopping. Even though he had to lean into the air to keep himself moving, he reached the twelve-foot mark where a perpendicular limb shot up like a staff. Then he paused to catch his breath and grin.

We gaped back, impressed by this elevated version of our father, glimmering like a statue on its pedestal. He held onto the vertical branch for support, weighing his options. He could come down now, having proved himself, or he could reach for even more glory.

"Da-ad?" I cautioned, guessing what he had in mind, which only goaded him into going further.

He leaned away and lunged around the vertical branch, putting his foot to the other side. He had not lunged enough, though, so he was stuck with one foot on the lower side of the branch, one foot on the higher, and all his top-heavy bulk leaning into space. Too late, he realized that the thin vertical branch that he was holding was dead. With a loud crack, it snapped away, and he had only enough time to squat, throwing his arms around the trunk as he rolled to one side.

For a second Dad's big sturdy legs scrabbled for a hold, and it looked as though he might stop the fall and right himself. Then he continued to slip around the huge slanted trunk like a rider slipping under a bull. All nobility disappeared. He was a cartoon caricature suspended by arms and legs. And because the trunk was simply too wide to grasp, he could not hold on for long.

He dropped flat-out, back-first, from twelve feet up, which meant he was unable to see what lay below and unable to protect anything vital. He fell so quickly and heavily that we were stunned by the sound as much as the sight. With a deep *whump*, the heft of his body hit the trickle of creek water and lifted a muddy geyser. The thump was so hard the ground trembled.

Paralyzed, we stared at our now-inert father, who was not moving a limb, his head nestled in a cup of mud.

When we ran toward him in panic, I was wondering, would he still be alive? And if he was, would he be a cripple the rest of his life like the star football player in town who had stepped off a roof accidentally?

He lifted a hand to keep us away, which seemed like a good sign. But he didn't say a word, which was bad.

"Are you okay?" we whispered, and he didn't answer, maybe having broken the apparatus that made speech possible.

Carefully, ponderously, he twisted himself onto his side and lay awhile, apparently trying to remember how to breathe. He attempted another movement, this time placing his hands in the mud and hoisting himself into a bowing, half-kneeling position.

"Are you okay?" we asked again, and still he didn't answer.

At last he stumbled to his feet, leaning over, shaking his head but not as if hearing our question. When he looked up at the tree, he seemed amazed, like a man stepping out of a grave. Then he lowered his head, shoulders trembling. He looked as if he might be crying, which caused us to stare at each other in horror. But no. Dad was laughing—laughing a breathy laugh that went on and on.

Half-relieved, half-afraid, we laughed along, looking at each other to make sure it was okay.

When he turned toward us at last, he was grinning. "So, boys, that's how it's done."

Cold Storage

Mom and my brothers had no energy, but I said yes, I would go. While my father gathered boots and gloves and a lumberman's hat with earflaps, I yanked on a black stocking hat of the sort with mouth and eyeholes. I rolled up the holes, knowing I could roll them down if necessary.

The snow had piled up eight inches deep on the lawn, so the first thing I did was to dive and tumble down the front yard. Then Dad and I tromped away toward the highway that ran the edge of town.

It was strangely quiet out there because the trucks had stopped across the river in St. Joe. The drivers were hunkered in motel beds watching Johnny Carson and waiting for daylight and snowplows. For a while, I just stood in the middle of the four lanes beside my father, watching flakes drift down under the streetlights, feathery flakes that fell slowly in the windless silence. I felt awkward but excited, not used to being so alone with my father.

The two of us walked further, turning onto a gravel road where our boots were muffled by thicker snow. The rocks were so buried I could not feel them underfoot.

"It's a blizzard, isn't it?" I declared.

"Not quite," said Dad. "If it was a blizzard, we couldn't see."

Since the snow wasn't blowing, we didn't have to squint. Even with the moon obscured by a thin layer of clouds, the white ground glimmered. As we walked, I could make out everything in silhouette: tree branches and barbed wire, even spikes of dried grass.

"I'll tell you who knew about blizzards," said my father. "Your granddad. Once he got lost and might have died except he found a fence and followed it home."

This mention of Grandpa and death brought back, with a sad pang, the fact that the sturdy old man with the white shock of hair and black eyebrows was no longer living. I thought of him reciting his favorite poem at the fiftieth wedding anniversary, a poem about a Yukon gold digger who insisted, on his deathbed, that he be cremated so he could get warm. I was surprised my dad was talking about his deceased father out here in the dark, since he had hardly mentioned him since the funeral.

"They had to amputate one of your granddad's toes," Dad said, which made me take stock of my own feet. They seemed fine in the felt liners of my boots.

My fingers ached a bit in my pockets but not enough to worry.

I looked out at the white fields and the black brush, and I could see everything in detail, like a line drawing. It was that way even after we had gotten over the next hill, away from all the lights of town. When a bird dashed out of the bushes, long necked and pointy, I could see the little crest on its head as it ducked under the fence.

"Pheasant," whispered my father, who had stopped to see if there might be more.

The two of us waited side by side, hearing nothing but our breath, and Dad began to describe very quietly how he had once gone hunting for pheasants with his father when he was thirteen. He said they had left the house before sunrise on a frigid day. The gun barrel was so cold in his hands that it hurt even with gloves on. He couldn't keep from complaining, walking on his heels, insisting his toes would fall off.

"I was miserable," Dad murmured, "until the sun came up, which made the grass look like it was burning. That's the part I remember best. I think you would have liked it."

"Yeah," I whispered, happy to be included, but I didn't add anything because I didn't want to stop the way that my father was talking. When we started to walk again, I waited for him to pick up where he had left off, letting memories spill out in a quiet church-voice, as if the night and the snow had opened some hidden storage.

"You know, your granddad always said after we moved to Kansas, that it just wasn't cold enough. If I complained, he told me I hadn't seen nothing. North Dakota, he said. Now *that's* cold."

"Maybe he liked all that cold when he was little," I said.

"I don't know..." Dad replied, his breath puffing out of him. "He used to tell us that the nail heads froze inside his house. He would wake up, and there were little beads of ice all over the walls."

I stayed quiet, leaving room for more.

"Once they ran out of things to burn. They didn't have trees, you know. It was all prairie. And the trains couldn't get through because of the snow. When they went to town, there wasn't any coal, so they had to start burning boards and stuff. I think they burnt a chair... Or maybe not."

As I listened, I wondered how long Grandpa's family had gone on like that—a day or a week?—but I kept that thought to myself.

"I remember this," Dad added, "when the train came at last, they could see it from miles away. They could see the smoke from the stack, and they danced out there in the yard."

How could they dance, I wondered, if the snow was so deep? Wouldn't it have been more like wading or wallowing?

"They must have been really happy," I said.

"Yeah, I bet they were."

"So did you ever go walking," I asked. "You know, with your dad in the snow?"

My father was quiet awhile. "No, not that I remember. Dad only walked if there was a reason. A broken car or a job to do—like shooting a pheasant."

He was quiet a little longer, before patting me on the back. "What do you think? You ready to turn around?"

"Naw," I said, just as quick as I could. Even though my legs were tired from lunging through the deepening snow, I didn't hesitate: "I'm fine. I bet I could go another mile."

So we continued over the next hill, moving side-by-side into the wide-open dark.

Family Legends

If guests came to dinner and everyone got comfortable, attention was likely to swing toward the past. This happened, for instance, when our father was asked where he grew up and one of the guests realized he or she had lived in a neighboring town. Suddenly all the adults would start reminiscing about how different things were back then: Boy Scouts gathering scrap iron for the war effort, men sharpening razors on a strop, the ice man hoisting blocks for the icebox. And these references to an earlier childhood had a predictable effect on my brothers and me; we butted in, begging Dad to tell a story from when he had worked at the local dairy barn in high school.

"Tell them about backing over the barn door with a tractor," we would plead. "Or tell about accidentally pulling the rope that emptied the grain bin. No, tell about the German POW chasing everyone with a pitchfork after someone broke a hardboiled egg on his head."

We knew the stories so well that we could have told them ourselves, but that wasn't the point. This was *his* youth, not ours, and we loved to see him claim it back, becoming the boy he used to be. More than anything we loved to see him admit the accident-prone problem he had been.

Our dad was not afraid to become the fool; and while he assumed that role, we listened like a choir might sing—all in unison, creating a harmony others could join. Our favorite story was the one about what happened when he took a turn driving the hay wagon. After we got him going, we would sit back and watch for the guests' reactions, relishing how he described the heavy, dusty work and the relief that came with climbing up onto the saddle of the tractor and getting a break.

The breeze felt great up in front of the wagon, he said, as it dried the dusty sweat on his arms.

"There was one guy up top, stacking bales," he explained, "and it was impressive how high he could get, sort of surfing up there on the pile. My job was to keep the tractor at a steady rate so he could balance okay and so the walkers could stay in step, throwing the bales to him or to the middle man on the floor of the wagon."

He usually stopped for a second and asked a question to get the audience fully hooked: "But what do you think? How long would that be exciting? I mean to drive a tractor in a hayfield in the middle of a Kansas summer?"

We knew the answer, of course, but we didn't say anything because we wanted the guests to get the pleasure of figuring it out. Someone usually guessed that it couldn't stay entertaining for too long, since the wagon had to move slowly and there weren't any turns except at the end of rows.

"Exactly," our father would say, thumping the table and flaring his eyes. "You put your finger on it. And why didn't they think of that when they invented the tractor, that's what I want to know. They could have added extra gadgets. Crossword puzzles on a flip-out clipboard. Drum sets. Typewriters. But did they take the driver's situation into account? Not a bit!"

He leaned back from the table and frowned. "So what was I supposed to do? Breeze is nice and all, but after an hour of letting the tractor idle, not even touching the throttle, what would any driver do?"

"I don't know," one of the guests might say, having learned that getting involved was allowed. "What would a driver do?"

"I'll tell you what. There was really only one thing that was of any interest when driving that tractor. You didn't need to steer hardly, and you weren't supposed to touch the clutch, just keeping her in the lowest gear. At the end of the row you'd make a slow, wide turn, but that was like sleepwalking. The only thing of interest were the handbrakes on the back wheels. If you pulled one of those, you could make the tractor do a U-turn. The foreman said we shouldn't do that because we'd jackknife the wagon. But he had never said anything about pulling *both* of the handbrakes at once."

"Oooh, not a good idea," one of the guests usually said, which was the sort of encouragement Dad loved.

"Exactly," he replied, pointing at whoever had recognized the folly of his thinking. "And sitting here at the dinner table, it's clear enough. But what if you'd been out there for hours on end—in 97 degree heat, no cab to give you shade, just the sun beating down on your head making you addled? What if you had a small case of heat exhaustion and you were so bored you couldn't even remember there were other people working behind you? Then what?"

"So what *did* you do?" the guest asked, seeing now that our father was delaying on purpose.

"Well... when I reached the end of the next row, I decided not to be shy—to just take the bull by the horns so to speak. I yanked back on both of the brakes then observed how the experiment worked. I'd say it was a success. If immediate results are the measure of a good experiment, this one was a success."

The guests laughed, which made my brothers and me laugh. We were enjoying the other people enjoying the story.

"I learned a bunch of things all at once," he said. "First of all, friction is a lot more powerful than most people realize. When those brakes were applied together, it was a revelation. That tractor stopped like it had hit a full-grown oak.

"And the other thing I learned is that for each and every action there is an equal and opposite reaction. When the tractor stopped, it stopped the wagon, but the fellow up top who was stacking hay had an equal and opposite reaction. He kept moving. In fact, for a little bit, he flew. And while he was flying, he did a complete flip; 360 degrees in the air, before he came down straddling the wagon tongue."

"Ouch," said all the listeners in unison, singing like a choir behind their soloist.

"Did he try to kill you?" one of the guests asked.

"Judging from the look in his eyes, I think he might have done such a thing. But he wasn't moving too well. I'm not sure he was even speaking. I think he just said my last name in a high, kind of cracked voice."

All the listeners guffawed, slapping at the table and wiping their eyes. We laughed along, watching their faces to get all the pleasure we could get out of this moment when our father's story was appreciated more widely than just by us. We were not separate siblings while we sat and laughed. We were part of something bigger and better.

When they had calmed down a bit, someone finally asked, "So did you keep driving?"

"No, now that I think of it, I don't recall ever driving

that tractor again. I believe that might have been the last time, which is probably just as well, since there wasn't much to do up there anyway."

Obedience Class

My parents had gotten their ideas about child rearing from a manual that was second only to the Bible in sales. The famous pediatrician who wrote the book didn't think much of spanking, but he said if you have to do it, don't do it angry.

Well, they had to do it because it was biblical: "Spare the rod and spoil the child." However, in deference to the good doctor, they were careful not to spank when still upset—except, that is, on the rarest of occasions, such as when one of their sons did something as stupid as running to the edge of a canyon, despite shouted warnings, then leaping onto a flimsy fence, risking life and limb.

On most occasions, they exercised remarkable restraint, waiting to discipline after their ardor had cooled. In fact, sometimes they waited so long I could tell it was hard to complete the promised punishment. Still, they stayed true to their word because the wise pediatrician counseled consistency.

Over time they had learned that, if they were in a public place, a warning could be indicated surreptitiously with a thumb and forefinger bent into a zero, or an initial sentence could be indicated with a lifted index finger. In this quiet but effective fashion, they doled out discipline in all manner of complicated situations. Thus, I once racked up a record-breaking four-finger salute by kicking my younger brother Nat under a restaurant table then reverting to a spit wad shot from my drinking straw then trying to protest in front of the amused acquaintances who were paying for the dinner.

Early on, I received my spankings equally from either parent, but by the time of that record-breaking four-finger sentence, Mom had turned over most of the duty to my father, since she no longer wielded a strong enough arm. The consequence was an added psychological weight. My dad was not only more heavy-handed, but I usually had to wait longer for him to come home from work and mete out punishment. In the hours before those long-delayed spankings, I could almost sense him frowning from the distance. Punishment waited in the wings, souring whatever might happen on stage.

Especially painful, of course, were the spankings that fell on celebratory days, such as the spanking I got on the evening of my tenth birthday. Earlier that afternoon, I had wrestled with seven-year-old Nat over what channel to watch on TV, snapping the big plastic knob off our console—a stupid and immature thing for me to do on the day I turned a decade old. While I waited for Dad to come home from work, I hoped in a hopeless way that, because this was my own birthday, I might be exempt. Not so. After supper, I was taken up to my bedroom as usual, for the standard dispensation of justice.

"God loves you and we love you too," I heard after the swats had been counted out. And when my father returned downstairs, I stayed on my bed wondering how God really could love me, given how consistently I failed to be good.

For a long time I moped on the red-ribbed bedspread, considering whether I should just stay there and give up on the whole birthday routine. Why even try to be happy at such a moment? Then, just as I decided that the mature thing was to get up and go downstairs, I heard creeping on the steps. Suspecting that Nat, ever the cheerful brother, was about to leap out and try to lift me from my funk, I grabbed a pillow and slung it over the bookcase.

As that pillow arced up and over the bookcase, I was alarmed to hear my whole family ease into a familiar chorus "Happy birthday to youuu... ." Then the song broke off and there was a cry from Mom. My older brother John called out, "Way to go, dude!"

To my horror, when the group emerged from the staircase, I saw that the pillow had fallen right across my birthday cake, bending back the pole-vaulting figure my mom had made from an action figure and a drinking straw. How bitter it was to have this failure added to the earlier one. There was no reproach, no additional swats. Dad even joked about how the pole-vaulter had scratched on his first attempt and would need a second try. I laughed along, trying to look amused as Nat licked icing off the pillowcase. However, inside I was not laughing. After I had unwrapped the BB gun I had gotten for a present, I simply could not enjoy it.

What I kept thinking that night, even after everyone had gone to bed, was this: If I had not lost my birthday wish by snuffing the candles, then maybe I could have wished to start the whole day over, returning to before I wrestled with my little brother and snapped the knob off the TV. If only I could start over again, maybe I could come back to this moment a wiser, better boy.

The Initiation

Turning thirteen—a word that ended with "teen"—meant arriving. It was time for my father-son trip.

John had already taken such a trip, canoeing on the border of Canada. He had come back with tanned, mosquito-bitten biceps, linked to our father by experiences that were theirs alone. Now it was my turn, and my first responsibility was deciding where to go. To my surprise, Dad said I could pick almost any place, whether Yosemite or the Everglades, so I flipped through a coffee-table book on touring America, trying to imagine myself snorkeling over a reef, spelunking in a maze of tunnels, or shouting on a snowy peak. For some reason, though, I kept coming back to a simple desire to camp where I had always camped—at the plywood shack a farmer had let us build in the woods near the bluffs of the Missouri River.

I knew that area well, down by the river, but I wanted to know it better. Trying to decide on a plan, I got out an antique county map my parents had bought from the pharmacy on Main Street, and I plotted some hikes I'd like to take, little excursions that would take us to places where settlements and farms used to exist three or four miles from our getaway shack.

I felt a bit ridiculous showing the marked map to my father, but he didn't hesitate. "Sure," he said. "If that's what you want, let's do it."

So that's how we ended up on a wooded hill a few weeks later, looking for an abandoned cemetery. The old plot was indicated on the newsprint map, just between our camping site and a river town that had burnt to the ground in the 1880's. After an hour and a half, we still hadn't found the cemetery and I was beginning to wonder if I shouldn't have picked the Everglades, but then the two of us realized simultaneously that we had walked right into the hidden site, now overgrown with dogwood saplings. Even up close it was impossible to recognize, since the iron fence had been toppled and many of the stone markers were moss-covered or snapped off.

Dad and I hooted and began rubbing at the lichen-covered faces of the faded stones, trying to read them. When I scraped a handful of dirt across the worn letters, it brought them back to life, telling of a Civil War soldier who must have died in battle, then three smallpox children lost in one year and a family killed by housefire. I shook my head, sobered by so much pain but also awed by the sheer drama of the past. So much history. Right here, under our very feet.

After thirty minutes, we hiked a bit beyond the cemetery, following barely discernible ruts of an abandoned road, and when it crowned a final ridge, we gazed down at the wide silver ribbon of the Missouri River. We could see the ruins of an old plantation house down there, perhaps all that was left of the town that had burnt a few years after the map was made, so we were lured down through the trees.

A few stone walls remained, roofless now and cluttered with rotting shingles; and about twenty yards away a double row of giant pines marched across a quarter-mile of bottom land toward a jetty, pointing the way to where steamboats must have docked. No doubt, the farmer of this house had hauled his corn and tobacco out to that landing, and no doubt his wife had purchased supplies like the Mason jar Dad discovered behind the house in a caved-in cellar.

The jar had green mottled glass and said "Patent 1858". It made me think of pickles and boiled beets. Excited, I dug deeper under the thrown-back door of the collapsed cellar, prying with an iron fence rod until I uncovered a second bottle: an elegant aqua bottle shaped like the arch of a stained-glass window and embossed with the strange title "Uncle Sam's Nerve and Bone Liniment."

Treasure. This was what I thought. And I became

ecstatic. To me the ruins of the plantation house and the cemetery were the landlocked equivalent of sunken ships, and my Dad and I were divers plunging into the land.

That night, excited by all we had seen, I couldn't stop talking by the campfire, imagining settlers who would have crossed into Kansas on the ferry at St. Joseph, Missouri, fifteen miles to the southeast. I could practically see them rattling past the plantation house in their boxy covered wagons, headed west to where Pawnee Indians waited on the horizon. History had come alive, conjured by the abandoned cemetery stones and the antique bottles. I could imagine a firm mother massaging liniment along the sore shin of her daughter or a tired family gathered round the Mason jar in the dead of winter, savoring sugary beets.

If allowed, I would have leapt right back into random exploration the next morning. However, my father announced an unexpected demand. When we had hardly climbed out of the plywood bunks in our shack and were huddled over the smoky sticks that snapped in the firepit, Dad said, "Here's the deal. I've got just one thing I want to do before we go out exploring. I want us to take thirty minutes for a shared devotional."

I grimaced. A devotional? That was something my parents did before I woke every morning, a solitary ritual that seemed to have nothing to do with turning thirteen or camping in the woods. The few times I had stumbled out of bed early enough, I had found Mom and Dad in separate armchairs, completely silent, either underlining verses on the tissuey pages of their Bibles or staring out the picture window into the dawn light as if waiting for something I couldn't see or hear. What did this completely quiet, completely stationary routine have to do with camping or searching for buried treasure?

"C'mon, Dad!" I implored. But he insisted, "Non-negotiable. There are only two rules for the father-son trip. First: You get to choose whatever we do. Second: We have a brief devotional each morning."

As a result, after we had eaten some fried eggs and washed the skillet, I begrudgingly took the brand new Bible that he handed me in a brown, faux-leather zipper case. "You're going to be a man soon," he said, "and a man has to have a plan for life, a direction to go. Here's your guidebook, your map."

A strange map, I wanted to say. Created thousands of years ago in some place I'd never been! I was still frustrated to have this formal exercise inserted into my day, as if a schoolteacher had hijacked our vacation. I was struggling with resentment as I scrambled down the creek bank with the zipped-up Bible and a notepad. But by the time I had climbed the far bank, whacking nettles out of the way with a stick, I became more peaceful, almost happy to be alone with my thoughts.

I climbed into the crook of a cottonwood that stood

in a clearing. Up there with the waxy leaves rattling, green on top and silver underneath, and with a hawk circling overhead, I felt remarkably aware. I opened the new Bible, smelling the still-drying ink, and read through the passage my father had assigned: "I am the true vine, and my Father is the gardener. He cuts off every branch in me that bears no fruit, while every branch that does bear fruit he prunes, so that it will be even more fruitful..."

I paused then looked out into the blue sky, out over the last ridge of trees to a shiny swathe of the Missouri River. This passage was kind of scary. I was no dummy, so I knew what was being said—"Without God, you're in big trouble." It seemed awfully foreboding on a bright Kansas morning.

On the other hand, I was intrigued to think of ancient Jewish vines and branches while sitting in a tree in the Twentieth Century. Even though Israel was on the other side of the globe and Jesus had lived two thousand years ago, I could identify with the chosen passage better up here than in a church pew. God had started everything in a garden, after all. And here was Jesus headed to another garden—Gethsemane.

"No branch can bear fruit by itself," he had said. "It must remain in the vine." But what kind of vine was he talking about? What kind of vine would he have actually known? Something like the unkempt grape vine my father and I had found by the caved-in plantation house?

I remembered, now, how we had plucked some of the pebbly fruit that dangled from a tangle of cord-like creepers along a fence. After polishing those dusty grapes on my shirt, I had popped them into my mouth, puckering. Even now, their tart flavor was with me, giving me a way to imagine the ancient grapes in the story, where they must have hung from branches that were connected to a thick vine, the sort that sprouted like a woody sapling.

Already this trip, so close to home, seemed rich with its own exotic fruit. It had an intense new taste. Though these verses had a dark edge to them, I liked that my father wanted me to think. In a bit I'd go talk with him, and I'd ask what about all the people in other countries who had no way to even know about Jesus, the ones living where no one read Bibles? How could it be fair for God to expect them to be connected in the same way?

I wasn't completely convinced, but right now I was full of quiet delight. Sitting in that cottonwood, with the leaves rattling and the hawk gliding overhead, I at least felt connected to my father and—through him—to the world around me, even to God, wherever God was. So I got out my pocket knife and chiseled a few letters and numbers into the tree bark: JOHN 15:5. I had a fine time imagining some farm boy finding that chiseled message thirty years from now, wondering what in the heck? Maybe it would feel like me finding the hidden gravestones on the hill. I hummed while I worked, not realizing until after I climbed down, that I had been humming a hymn.

Living with Saints

When we went to visit Grandma Lillian, after she sold the house where my dad grew up and moved to a retirement center, people would realize who we were. At the grocery store, if we were buying sherbet to go with Grandma's 7-Up, the woman at the register would see the last name on the check and say, "Oh my, you must be related to Doc K.F." Or at the gas station when the mechanic was holding the credit card by its edges trying not to get it greasy, he would say, "Whoa, there. Are you some of Doc Bascom's folks?"

Even though Grandpa had been dead five years now and was retired for ten years before that, he had been one of the first doctors in Manhattan, Kansas, and he had become a pillar for the community, helping to form the local historical society, creating a scholarship fund for students who wanted to study science, even walking in the cancer fundraiser after being diagnosed with stage three cancer.

Everyone seemed to share the same respect. “He was a true gentleman,” they would declare. “I never heard a bad word about that man.”

Sometimes, though, these people weren’t talking about my grandfather; they were referring to my uncle George, who had returned to the same town and opened a surgery practice alongside Grandpa. Uncle George was already taking on his own legendary status, even though alive and kicking. Thankful former clients would confide about him driving to a farmhouse in a weekend blizzard to see if a child might have appendicitis or stitching up a spouse who had flown through a windshield. They praised the hospice program he had established and how he would still come by to see dying patients when surgery had failed.

“I’ve never met a doctor who cared more,” the lady at the florist said, as my parents picked out Mother’s Day flowers for Grandma. “You know, after my mom was diagnosed with the cancer, Doc Bascom came down here with cherry pie. He didn’t have to do that; it’s just the way he is.”

She lowered her voice then, so other customers couldn’t hear. “I remember when his oldest passed away—you know, with the pills and all. What a shame. The whole town was shocked. But sometimes the Good Lord can turn the worst situation into a blessing. I think that’s what opened him up. With Doc, you always feel like he understands no matter what. You folks are lucky just to be related."

As I listened that summer before junior high, I was prone toward inexplicable emotions, and I had several tumbling around inside me. Naturally, I was proud. It was thrilling to come to this bigger town, practically a city, and have so many people showing respect—all because of a shared last name! But there was also a pressure that went with this name. I hadn't earned such respect, so I felt a twinge of guilt—and a need to prove myself. At the florist shop I found myself trying out the expression "Yes ma'am." Then when we were leaving, I found myself curiously compelled to hold the door for an in-coming customer.

There was another, even more troubling emotion, too. I felt a kind of frustrated envy because no one here seemed to realize that my own dad was a doctor. Maybe he wasn't a surgeon like Grandpa or Uncle George, but he was still a doctor, and back in our own town people called him "Doc" too, treating him with great esteem.

The people here had no idea about this hidden parallel. And if they realized, they looked shocked. "You gotta be joking!" they proclaimed. They even burst out laughing as if this was too absurd to be true.

"Well I guess the nut doesn't fall far from the tree," said the florist, which made it seem as if my grandfather and uncle were the center of everything and Dad was an inconsequential object dropped to the side.

I thought I could see my father's smile go slack as

the woman wrapped the flowers and handed them over. I thought I could see a weariness around his eyes, like smoke. It made me want to say something out loud, telling the woman about the night my father had driven all the way to the edge of our county to console Edna, not returning till past midnight even though he knew the old widow's chest pains were mere loneliness. It made me want to tell the florist how my father had once given his own blood for an emergency patient, since there wasn't any available of that type.

In the car on the way to Grandma's apartment, Mom said, "Well, that was sweet. She sure thinks a lot of your brother." And I watched as Dad nodded quietly. I also noticed, when we crossed the parking lot at the retirement center, how he picked up a pop can that had been tossed on the grass. I noticed how he jogged forward to help an elderly man carry groceries into the center. And how heartily he held out the daisies for his mother, telling her, "Thanks for bringing me into the world, Mom—and putting up with so much imperfection."

My uncle was already in the apartment, along with his wife, and he hugged Dad. He had brought flowers as well—a set of roses—and the apartment smelled thick with their velvety scent. This big smiling man took a sideways hug from each of us boys, commenting on how much taller I looked—practically five-foot-three, he guessed. Then, since I had to pee, I went to the bathroom, passing Mom and my aunt, where they had followed Grandma Lillian into the kitchen.

When I came back out, I remembered my resolution to be worthy of the family name, so I stopped and asked if I could be of help. My grandmother looked surprised, but she nodded: "Why not? You can bring the caramel rolls as soon as they're ready." Then she disappeared with several floats of 7-Up and lime sherbet.

I waited beside Uncle George's wife while Mom forked rolls onto plates and added scoops of vanilla ice cream. I listened as this aunt, Jane, complained about her husband not returning from work in time to go to an opera that was happening over at the state capitol. "An appendectomy is always a good excuse," she quipped, in her ever-blunt way.

Jane picked absentmindedly at the corner of her scarlet lips, and I noticed a nicotine-stain on her finger, a sign that she was smoking again.

My mother sighed in sympathy, but I could tell it was the sort of sigh she gave if she was not fully convinced. "It's tough being a doctor's wife, isn't it?" she said. "I don't think people realize; doctors are such public property."

"And always saving the world," said my aunt, "which, of course, means everything else is second priority."

"What's a person to do?"

"Not a damn thing. Just stand back and applaud."

Mom laughed in a shocked, high voice, like a sudden

shift in a wind chime. "It's not that bad, is it?"

"I swear it is. I can't go to a place without hearing about how good a man my husband is, which of course raises the question, what sort of person am I?"

There was an awkward pause before she went on: "It's not easy, you know, to constantly play accompaniment. He may be a saint, but people have no idea how hard it is to live with a saint."

At this point my mother glanced over, seeming to notice me for the first time. "Here," she said, "you'd better take these plates in."

So I took the caramel rolls and ice cream, and I walked back into the living room, where Nat and John were grinning at a joke that my uncle was telling about a Norwegian (not a Swede like us) who was hired to paint lines on a road with a brush. This big oaf of a Norwegian did a great job on his first day, painting over a mile, but the next day he was down to half that distance, and the next day half of half. And when the fellow was completing only fifty yards of roadway in a day, the boss had to tell him he was fired.

"Ole," he said, "I can't tell you how disappointed I am. What's your problem, son? How could you go from painting a whole mile of road to painting only a few yards?"

"Well, boss," said Ole, completely tuckered out. "I'm sorry, sir. But it just keeps taking longer and longer to walk back to the bucket."

Ha!

I looked over as my father guffawed and wiped the corners of his eyes. I could tell he was not laughing just to be polite. He was laughing because he loved the joke and because he loved to see his brother tell a joke. He laughed so freely that I began to laugh along. I felt honored to belong to such a good family, to inherit so much. I felt an even stronger desire to be worthy of all this—to really make a life for myself. No, not for myself as much as others. That's it. I wanted to live in a way that would matter to those around me.

However, as I laughed along, I also remembered my Aunt Jane back in the kitchen, and the chagrin I had heard in her voice. "Be good," I imagined her whispering to me, "but be prepared to not be good enough."

Taking a Hit

I had played football in junior high, but I wasn't so sure about playing in high school. There were several ostensible reasons:

I would have afternoons to myself and could watch my favorite after-school TV shows like *I Dream of Jeannie* or *My Favorite Martian*.

I could, perhaps, get a job and start making money.

I could put off my homework because there would always be more time in the week!

But really the main reason was this: I had heard rumors about what happened to incoming freshmen. I had heard about dogpiling and extra drills and snapped towels in the showers. I had heard about de-pantsing too, and guys who got shoved into the dining hall half-naked.

So I was chicken, basically.

Then the high school coach approached me at the end of my eighth-grade year, when I was sent to the high school library to fetch a set of books. "See you at fall practices," he said, and I answered "Yeah," because I was afraid to say no to such a big, ruddy, sunburned man.

Sure enough, on the first day of practice—just after a heavy rain—the seniors chased down one of my classmates, tackling him in a mudhole. When Coach came onto the field and saw the state of this freshman—covered with mud from his cleats to the top of his helmet—he didn't show any compassion either. He didn't ask how this had happened, nor did he scold the smirking upperclassmen. He just looked at the kid with the splattered uniform and mud-speckled face then said, with disgust, "You Ding-a-Ling. Go home."

After that, I always took extra time in the locker room, removing thigh pads and knee pads from my practice pants so that I would have to re-insert them. I would re-adjust those pads until I saw Coach or his assistant headed for the door, and only then would I step outside, right on their heels.

Still, that couldn't rescue me from other dreaded scenarios, the worst being the end-of-practice whistle that signaled kick-off drills. Inevitably, Coach would send the "meat squad" onto the field as a receiving team, which meant I had to jog out there with all the second stringers—fellow freshmen and sophomore runts—and take my position in a corner behind this motley crew, hoping the first-string kicker would send the ball to the other corner, where the other freshman running back was probably thinking the exact same thing—*No, not me.*

Fifty percent of the time the ball came my direction, and just catching it was tough, since I could hear all those seniors and juniors stampeding toward me as the ball hung in the sky. But what was especially distressing was that the blockers up front tended to step aside as the starters came thundering downfield. They did not want to take a hit any more than I did—not from a guy who weighed thirty pounds more, could lift fifty pounds more, and could run the fifty yard dash in only six seconds.

Typically, I had about one-and-a-half seconds between cradling the ball and first contact. If I didn't drop it out of sheer terror, I tended to jump sideways, hoping to avoid a crushing hit. Then, if I succeeded at that, I had to at least act as if I was interested in getting to the far end zone, so I would zigzag toward the back of one of my supposed blockers, shadowing him as he looked over his shoulder. A second wave of heavier, slower starters arrived, so I reached out and rammed this reluctant blocker right into the first galloping opponent. Then I ducked the opposite direction, scrunching over the ball.

Coach blew the whistle after I was down. He scowled and told me to put some fight into it. However, this scared-rabbit routine was default for my first month of practice.

I didn't understand. As an eighth grader I had not been like this. I had been a tough, big guy who ran confidently. But now? I felt dwarfed and vulnerable, and I simply wanted to avoid pain.

What made the situation even more distressing was that I knew my father had been devoted to football, playing it with gusto. At the dinner table, I had heard him joke about coming to one of his first high school practices and hitting a tackling dummy so hard that it fell off its chain. I had heard him describe wanting so badly to stop a star running back that he threw his body across the galloping opponent, taking a knee in the side and rupturing his spleen. That was the fearless attitude I wanted to emulate, not this please-don't-hurt-me approach.

In practice, our coach often pitted the starting defense against the second-string offense. Then I might have to run the ball again, taking whatever hits the starters dished out. I was a fullback and got the ball less than the tailback, so I would step into the huddle praying for a fake. Eventually, though, I had no choice but to take a hand-off. The good news is that I tended to be sent straight up the middle, where the center and guards would collapse back into me and I would get wrestled to the ground before the high-speed linebackers arrived. Sometimes, though, I had to run a side route, and that was a more perilous scenario. For a bit I was exposed on my flank, and then I had to turn into a hole knowing that a linebacker was probably accelerating toward our inevitable collision.

One afternoon, our second string quarterback called a "Fake 32 Left 45," which meant doing one of these dreaded side routes. According to plan, I stepped to the right, lifting my forearms as if blocking. The quarterback faked a handoff to the tailback, who shot through. Then I pivoted 180 degrees and ran behind the turned-around quarterback, taking the hidden ball and heading toward the assigned hole just beyond the left tackle.

Usually, such a complicated play would get broken up early. We were the second string offense, after all. And if the play got broken up, I wouldn't have to turn up-field into the area patrolled by linebackers, which was fine, as far as I was concerned. However, today everything went almost too well. No one touched me, and I still had the ball when I got to the designated hole.

I could see several yards of possible progress—all that was really required of me as a fullback. However, a linebacker was barreling into that open space at a gallop, so I hesitated.

This particular linebacker was one of the biggest guys on the starting team and one of the meanest. He was a bully really, known to punch smaller guys just for the hell of it. He had broken the arm of an opposing player in the first game of the season. And when I saw him coming, I did *not* turn into the hole and try to get those couple yards. Instead, I started running sideways, hoping to get around the end of the line.

A huge mistake. I had only taken a couple steps when the linebacker broke through the hole and dove into me, lifting me right off my feet and smashing me down onto the ground. I hit so hard on my chest that all the air went out of me, and my facemask dug into the turf, trapping a divot of dirt.

After the other guy got up, I just lay there face-down, feeling like I had when my older brother had practiced boxing with me, years ago, and hit me in the solar plexus. My lungs were switched off. Coach had to turn me over, face-side up, and lift me by the belt to get air moving again. And then I had dirt in my mouth, dropping out of the divot that was trapped in my facemask.

Coach, with his permanently sun-burnt face and chapped lips, just shook his head in that sorrowful way that meant he couldn't believe the complete uselessness of this half-hearted freshman.

"What were you thinking, you dip-shit? We didn't call a sweep. No one told you to run around the end. When there's a hole, go into the hole. Follow the frickin' play."

Something very interesting happened in that moment, there on the ground with the coach looming over me, mocking me. First of all, I got quite embarrassed, which I didn't like. Then I got really angry. I was tired of this whole ridiculous protect-yourself attitude. It had done nothing for me except make life miserable. Now I had gotten what I feared, and so, in some sense, it was over with. It couldn't get worse.

After I had pulled some air back into my lungs and after I had stood up, I spat the dirt out of my mouth and decided I was through with the old approach. I was going to run the ball as hard as I could. I was going to run it straight into anyone who stood in my way because, if evading a tackle hurt this much, what did I have to lose from *not* evading a tackle?

So the next time I was assigned the ball, I did just as I had promised. It was a "42 route," straight up the middle, and I crashed into the back of my own blocker then bounced off and crashed into a tackler. But instead of giving up, I kept my knees pumping, pushing for another yard. To my surprise I got three, actually making the defensive lineman fall backward.

I tried the same approach again on a surprise screen pass. After I had run out to the side and caught the ball, instead of heading toward the sidelines like usual, I ran right at the first defender and lowered my shoulder and smashed into him. Although the guy hung on and another tackler came to help, I kept pushing and fell on top of both of them, gaining another three or four yards. More importantly, it didn't hurt.

On the next running play assigned to me, one of

the starting defenders actually became agitated, not expecting to get pushed backwards. He growled through his mouthguard, “C’mon boy. Just go down!”

To hear this coming from one of the starting linebackers was a delicious surprise. It boosted my confidence. And so, after that, I started playing like I actually wanted to be on the team—like I was determined to make something out of this freshman season even if no one else expected it. And the feeling that I got was euphoric.

It’s strange; I may have come closer to a religious high out there on the field than I had ever come in church. In the weeks to follow, I stopped hiding in the locker room before practice. Sometimes, when I went out onto the field, I even whistled.

The Embarrassment Factor

Sometimes my father didn't seem to realize he was embarrassing me. Other times he seemed to know quite well, taking pleasure in the fact. Being embarrassed never killed anyone, he liked to say. Which made sense rationally but made no sense emotionally—not for a kid who was in high school for the first time and surrounded by bigger guys who were already starting to shave.

Take, for instance, the time my father arrived late for my first high school band concert then stood at the back of the auditorium waving his arms.

"Is that your dad?" asked the first and second trumpets as they set up their sheet music.

"Hey, dude, what's your old man doing?" asked the trombone while emptying his spit valve.

I acted like I couldn't hear, refusing to look up at the shadowy area behind the stair-stepped seating because I had already noticed my dad there, taking off his rain-spattered hat to whack it against his thigh. I realized he was getting comfortable back there, where no one could see him except my peers, most of them one or two year's older and therefore critical to impress. Only I and my fellow bandmates could see the silly wide-brimmed hat, so brightly checkered, like a starter's flag. Only we could see the long black jacket gaping as my father lifted his hat and waved it, looking like a flagman at a car race.

"Hey, Sweetcakes, what's your dad want?" whispered the cute senior flute player in front of me, but I shook my head, mortified. The way I shook it was meant to convey a lot of things: I can't believe this is happening, I don't want to talk about it, and yes that's my dad but could we please act like he's not.

The apple baskets were different, though. The first time one of the baskets appeared in my locker room after a junior varsity football game, no one knew where it had come from. All my teammates were tugging off their jerseys, teasing anyone who didn't have enough grass stains to prove they had taken a hit. Then Coach surprised us by announcing, "There's some apples here if anyone wants one."

Despite having been on the field for only a few plays (or maybe because of it), I really wanted one of those apples. It was a consolation of sorts. And I noticed that even the teammates who hadn't gotten into the game grabbed for an apple, munching as they peeled off the still-clean layers of their uniforms: thigh pads and girdle pads and T-shirts and jocks.

These were Jonathan apples, and they came in the kind of open box used at the fruit market that stood on the highway, just shy of the bridge into St. Joseph, Missouri. They were tart apples that burst when you bit. They seemed like an odd choice for a post-game snack—until I tasted one. It was better than anything I might drink, since it could be savored slowly, flavoring the back of my throat and taking away the parch without weighting my stomach.

Another basket showed up at the next game, making the apples into a kind of mystery that begged for solving. Coach wouldn't say who was the supplier, except to confess that he hadn't bought them himself.

Then, during the third or fourth game, a kid who went to the locker room to replace a broken chinstrap noticed a man walking up with another one of the apple baskets. "It was your old man," he said, pointing to me.

"Way cool," said the tailback. "Yeah," added our starting center, a big beefy guy with knees that bent in. "Tell your dad to keep 'em coming."

A couple other starters went out the door carrying their gym bags, still nipping at the pith around the cores. They called back, "Hey man, your dad rocks."

That night when I got home, I told my father what a hit he had made with the team.

"What are you talking about?" he asked, feigning surprise.

"Oh, I think you know."

He grinned widely. Then I told him that the guys wanted the tradition to continue.

I couldn't say what I really meant since it might sound sissy, but I hoped my father understood. I hoped he knew, without hearing it, that I was glad he was a bit different than some dads, not afraid to try something unusual or to stand out, not afraid to risk being an embarrassment now and then.

Sex Ed

As far back as third or fourth grade, I had occasionally gone with my father, the doctor, on rounds at the hospital. This was an education of sorts, taking me out of the little town where we lived and into the city, where a different sort of people lived, shopping at the mall if they felt like it, eating at the A & W, and watching movies every night at the movie theater that had three different screens. Even the waiting room in the hospital was enlightening, with a stack of magazines I had never seen in my home: gritty magazines with photos of weary soldiers coming back from Viet Nam, or glossy magazines with lots of ads for hair coloring and bras, just like the strappy white things I saw in the laundry basket but never on my mom, who glided from bedroom to bathroom in a terry cloth robe.

One day at the hospital, when I was probably only eight or nine years old, I was flipping through a magazine and came across a photo of a man standing behind a woman on a couch and slipping his hand inside her collar, burying it where one of her breasts was hidden. It was a strange picture, unlike anything I had seen before, so I studied it carefully. The man was grinning like he was playing an April Fool's joke, and the woman was mouthing a big "O," a little bit like my mom had done once when I put an ice cube down the back of her shirt.

There was a kind of mutual horseplay here that was unfamiliar to me as a third-grade boy. Yes, my father would sometimes place a hand on my mother's waist and lift her hand Fred-Astaire-style, like a dancer mugging for the camera. Or he might plant a stage-kiss on her waiting lips, reaching his face toward hers in a gesture that was pure symbol. But I had never seen anything so frank as this man and woman in the photo at the waiting room, which made me curious. Why would a man do such a thing?

It may have been that same afternoon—just as we crowned a hill in the Chevy Impala with sun glaring on the windshield—that a horn blared and Dad slammed the brakes so hard that I flew into the dashboard. A car shot through the intersection with the driver leaning out the window, and this other man shouted as he disappeared down the side street, "Fuck you," leaving those two words smeared in the hot tarmacky air.

After my father had eased across the busy intersection, I risked a question I wasn't sure I should ask. "Dad, what's 'fuck' really mean?"

There was a long silence, then a terse response, "Nothing you need to know right now."

Apparently, the need to know did not apply until five years later, when I was about to go into high school. Then one summer evening my father ushered me into the master bedroom for a private confab, promptly explaining all the mechanics of sex with words like testicles and vagina and ejaculation. He said the boys at school probably used dirty words to talk about this stuff, but sex was something beautiful, a special gift from God which shouldn't be unwrapped and enjoyed until marriage.

Before I could make a comment, Dad left me on the queen-size bed my parents shared—to listen to a tape by a minister who was an expert on this hitherto taboo subject. It was a jocular talk with a teenage audience that laughed at appropriately embarrassing moments. I listened awkwardly, picking at the puffballs that were strung along the edge of the bedspread. Only when the tape was done did my father come back to ask, "So... any questions?"

I did have one. My penis had been stirring in my pants a lot and getting stiff at unexpected moments—sometimes when I saw girls but sometimes even if I sat around in tight jeans. Was that normal?

Dad, a doctor, was all business. He said erections were to be expected when males reached puberty. He said the penis could seem almost out of control during those early teen years. "You may even wake up," he said, "and think you had an accident, but it's probably what we call a wet dream."

"Did it happen to you when you were my age?"

"Wet dreams?"

"No. Did you get erections a lot?"

My father looked at me with a half-smile, apparently not sure what to do with such candor.

"I used to get them quite a bit," he said. Then after a pause, "I remember once when I went to a dance, I got an erection while I was dancing a slow dance. I was afraid the girl would notice, so I had to dance the whole dance hugging her up top but staying away below."

This was a comfort to me—to know that my own father had gotten unexpected erections, so I didn't worry about them as much after that, except when I had to stand up in class and go to the board or walk around in the cafeteria where the change might be noticeable.

A few months later, at the second dance that I had ever gone to, a girl asked me onto the dance floor, and I shook my head. However, my friends shoved me out there, so I finally went, partly because I didn't want to be seen wrestling but partly because I actually wanted to go.

I danced a couple quick songs with her, jogging in

place and holding my arms out as if swinging invisible weights. I didn't know what to do, though, when the music went slow. The girl didn't turn away to join her friends, so I didn't. Then the only thing left to do was to step in and put my hands around her waist, which I had never done with a girl.

Though I held her loosely, my front slid across her front as we swayed. She seemed comfortable with all this touching, her arms around my neck. She let her breasts squeeze up against my chest. Then it began to happen: my penis perked. When I felt it grazing the front of her dress, I stepped back mortified, and this reminded me how my father had done the same thing thirty years ago. In fact, that strange recollection gave me just enough courage to stay put instead of running for the hallway door. I kept swaying right through the slow song, bent over toward the girl as if leaning over a wall. I kept leaning into her even though my lower back cramped slowly into a giant charley horse.

How amazing it was to feel so much energy rippling up and down my limbs and torso, causing me to shiver. For the first time, I understood why the man in the photo wanted to put his hand down the woman's shirt. It was a marvel—all that tingling energy that kept singing away inside me, as if I had filled up with a gentle but insistent electricity. It was frightening to be so alive, so close to a kind of bursting.

I held the girl very gingerly, as if she was a vase

that might shatter or as if she was something delicate on a pedestal. And when I walked back to my grinning friends on the gym bleachers, I felt like a different person altogether, no longer the boy who had shoved against them a few minutes ago, no longer pushing away from my future, instead ready to let it arrive.

The Father Who Was Once Sixteen

When I finally got my permit at the end of freshman year, I could drive to school alone. The problem was that the permit did not allow me to drive anywhere else on my own. As soon as classes ended for the summer, I needed to see my girlfriend. That's because in a few days she would be gone forever, moving to another state. Her father had taken a job at a seed company, so he was selling the family farm, five miles out of town.

During the first and second days of summer vacation, I waited impatiently, unable to get my mother to go with me since she was volunteering for a book sale at the town library. I waited through supper the next day, until finally, at dusk, my father agreed to accompany me.

As soon as I had turned the key, Dad had advice: "Always adjust the mirror."

Then, as we pulled up to the stop sign at the end of

the block, he added, "Look both ways."

"Dad, I know. It's not like I haven't driven before."

There were no vehicles coming, so I swung the car onto the main road and started out of town, leaving behind the streetlights that were flickering to life in the lowering night. The blacktop was empty. My headlights seemed dim in the dusk. And my father couldn't help himself: "If you want brights, hit the button on the floor."

"I know," I grumbled.

After a bit, Dad tried to make small talk, "Now, is this the girl who's such a fast runner?"

"Yeah."

"Didn't she even beat the seniors this year?"

"Yeah."

I offered no more, though. The connection to my girlfriend had formed slowly and always somewhere else than home, such as the town pool, the 4-H fair, or the high school track. I knew my dad was trying to show interest the way that fathers show interest, but I was not convinced that he, as an older man, could appreciate who my girlfriend was nor the depth of what I was going through—the almost panicky grief that swept over me when I thought about her imminent departure. She was being forcibly taken away, and I felt betrayed. In some vague way I blamed all adults for the lack of control I had.

"We can't stay past 9:00," my father said.

"C'mon, Dad, that's hardly an hour."

"People go to bed at 9:00. Especially farmers."

I glanced over to frown at him, and I saw him smiling in the dim light. It was the same secretly amused smile I had seen back at the house when I was impatient for the family to finish supper, so it made me mad. I was not trying to be cute here. This was not just puppy love. I knew the difference because in eighth grade I had gone through a silly fling. A pretty girl from the seventh grade had seen me looking at her through the doorway between our classrooms and she had mouthed the words "Do you like me?" Since her lips seemed soft and her eyes remarkably blue, I had said yes. I didn't want to hurt her feelings, after all. But with this high school girlfriend, two years later, I didn't just like her; I could feel my senses hum every time I rounded a corner and spotted her. It wasn't just her cockeyed grin or the cascade of fine sandy hair. It wasn't the upright way that she walked. It was something about the way she looked back at me—as if saying yes, always yes.

Though I had known this girl for years, sharing classes through grade school and junior high, something inexplicable changed during track season of our sophomore year. I first realized it when we were at an "away" track meet and the two of us found ourselves alone, lounging on the grass while our friends competed in other events. Nothing I said was different from the way I usually talked to her, but the girl looked back as if she was storing each sentence inside—as if she would be happy to stay right there and keep understanding me all afternoon.

On the bus that evening, as we shared one of the bench seats in the dark, I had an uncontrollable urge to take her hand, so I did, pulling it into the pocket of my windbreaker, where her fingers intertwined with mine in a secret tryst. Then, a few days later, when track practice got rained out, I waited with her until her dad came to pick her up, putting my arm around her shoulder as we sat under the eaves.

We leaned together for warmth while the rain hammered against the eaves and cascaded down in a sheet. When it suddenly stopped, there were crystal-like beads clinging to the lettuce and the rhubarb and the row of roses around the perimeter of the Home-Economics garden. Discussion had become a bit self-conscious, affected by our nerves and adrenaline, but now we sat in peace, confident of our connection, which I could almost hear like a hum, a pleasant ringing at some wavelength only the two of us shared.

Our faces were close together. She looked at my lips, so I found the courage to come closer. We touched mouths, soft flesh against flesh, and I tasted her breath, musky and full of a kind of unfolding velvet. It was like a whole new world opened to me.

After that kiss, every day seemed like an amazing exploration full of potential discoveries. I woke with relish, ready to go to school. I came down to breakfast without being prompted. I had entered a realm where it seemed that no one else had gone—the first to see, the first to enjoy. My delight didn't end until noon-time a month later when my girlfriend, eyes welling with tears, pulled me out to the parking lot during lunch break and told me that her father had taken a new job across the river in St. Joseph.

That terrible announcement is what I was thinking about as I turned onto the gravel road that led to her farm with the headlights of the family car sweeping over ghostly cottonwoods. I figured that my dad, sitting right there beside me, thought I was too young to be so serious about a relationship, and I had the urge to speak out loud, telling him that maybe the reverse was true: Maybe he himself had become too old to remember what love really felt like. I mean, how could my father relate? Now he was in his forties, accustomed to having an unshakable wife at home. She wasn't leaving him to live in the next state. She would be right there in the house when we returned tonight. What the two of them had, by now, was probably more assumption than anticipation.

As was the custom at most farms, there was a dog—actually two—which came barking as soon as the car had pulled up to the house. A black Labrador and a spotted Spaniel jumped onto the car doors as my girlfriend came out of a side door and called them off.

She took my hand when her parents stepped out. She held on, and I could feel an electric charge coming from her—a kind of tingling energy that coursed up my arm.

To my surprise, her parents suggested, "Why don't you two take a walk while we have some coffee." I was relieved. I had feared there would be no privacy.

After we had strolled to the barn behind the house, where the two dogs circled and brushed our legs, we swung into each other's arms and stood in a long embrace. We were out of the brightly-lit circles under the yard lights. The barn was on a small rise, so we could not only see the rectangles of light from the kitchen and bedroom windows but the far away windows of another farmhouse gleaming through a hedge row. Those lights were beautiful from where we stood, glittering in the distant dark.

I kissed her long and slow, as if drinking her in. This was not a lascivious tongue-twining kiss. It was the pure kiss of someone who wanted to be close to someone else. It was the innocent kiss of someone who didn't need anything more than a kiss.

Then we talked about things that had happened in the days since school got out: How she had gone one last time to fish in her farm pond and hooked a six-pound channel cat, or how I had built a go-cart with my younger brother who had tried to ride it in the rain and got thrown right off when his plastic poncho caught in the spokes of a wheel.

We laughed, attempting normalcy, but I was terribly aware that everything about our normal existence was going to change. She seemed aware, too. We lapsed into silence, then more kissing, and she said at last, "Don't you think we should go back?"

Later that evening, after I had let my father take the wheel, too despondent to drive, I shrank back as he tried to engage me in conversation.

"So her folks seem like good people."

"I suppose."

I didn't want to let Dad into the private space where I was still holding onto my girlfriend and lamenting the inevitable loss. When he asked how she was doing, I just muttered, "Okay, I guess."

"And how about you?"

"Just great, Dad."

I knew he was reaching for me, trying to be sensitive, but I still couldn't trust him. What did my father expect me to say under such circumstances? Yeah, I'm doing wonderful—except for when I feel like I'm on Death Row waiting for execution?

There was a long silence before my father spoke again, "Well, maybe we can get the two of you together again."

"When?"

"I don't know. How about this weekend?"

"Dad, they leave on Friday."

"Well, I can't get you over there for a day or two. The car's scheduled for maintenance."

I sighed heavily, as if this slight was too much to bear. I sighed as if my father was trying to punish me. Then I was surprised by his cryptic response: "You know, I was sixteen once."

"What's that supposed to mean?"

"I mean there was a time when I was sixteen, too."

We were both quiet after that. Dad made no effort to explain, and I sat in silence. To my own discomfort, it occurred to me that thirty years ago my dad might have been in love like I was. No doubt, he had kissed some girl who was not my mother. No doubt, he had longed for that girl the way I longed for my girlfriend. In fact, it was possible he had even lost that other girl after she had to move away.

It was frightening to think like this. My father seemed so adult in relation to my mother—playful yes, affectionate occasionally (in a lean-over-and-give-her-a-peck sort of way), but not passionate like someone who was living for the next contact. So I was stunned to think that he might have once felt emotions just as powerful as my own, might have wanted to drink some girl in so that she could never be taken away.

As we drove down the last hill before town, entering back under the streetlights, I was reminded of something I had realized a long time ago when looking into a bathroom mirror: A father was also a son on some level—always not just a middle-aged man, but a teen, just like myself.

The next day, when I asked my dad for a ride to my girlfriend's house, I asked differently—as if he might want to help. In fact, he *did* help. He rescheduled the car maintenance and, instead of taking me to the girl's house, he arranged for her to come to our home. She stayed the whole day. She ate lunch with me and my brothers and my mother. She stayed for supper and played Monopoly with the whole family. And that night, she came up to my bedroom to lie beside me on the bed just looking into my eyes between kisses, just listening to the hum of connection that was ours alone.

Though I was devastated when at last she left, and though I felt despondent after each telephone call I made to her at her new home in Missouri, I did not shut my father out when he asked, "So, how is she doing?" Instead, I tried to find a way to answer, to at least acknowledge that he *might* actually understand.

Follow the Leader

"Are you sure they said Schloss Klaus?" my mother asked, wondering whether the train was headed the right direction.

"No problem," Dad replied, his voice too loud again, which made me—a seventeen-year-old—cringe.

The other passengers, all Austrian, were staring straight ahead, but they seemed too alert, as if tuning in surreptitiously. I was conscious that every word my mother shouted to my half-deaf father made the family appear more foreign and confused. No one else was talking loudly. No one else was blocking the aisle with suitcases or unfolding a gargantuan map of Europe.

My brothers had taken the available booth-seat across from my parents. Instead of standing by them, I stepped back two rows and took an empty seat next to a gray-headed gentleman in corduroys, whose neatly trimmed sideburns gave him a long, dignified face. Even from there, I could hear Mom trying to be heard over the whine and rattle of the train: "If we're going east, shouldn't the sun be behind us?"

"Relax," said my father. "The train probably turns outside the city."

This was only the third day of our European vacation, and it had already turned sour for me, despite the fact—or perhaps due to the fact—that I was about to start my senior year at high school and would soon be out on my own, going to college. I chafed at the agenda my parents had set for us and the way my older brother John kept persuading them to adjust, having more influence because he was the oldest. I also resented the little history lessons that John trotted out, back from his second year of college, where he had learned all about the Austro-Hungarian Empire and the Republic that replaced it after World War I and then the short dictatorship of some self-appointed dictator named Dolfuss, who went wooing Benito Mussolini—that is, if my brother had any idea what he was talking about.

When John started to bring up yesterday's tour of Salzburg, where we had seen the film sites used in *The Sound of Music*, he spoke as if he had been right there in the concert hall while it was filmed, singing along on "Edelweiss."

Blossom of snow may you bloom and grow, I thought, biting the words off as I stared out the window at forested mountains and green glades speckled with wildflowers. I thought of Captain von Trapp, who could be so severe, even cruel, yet never gauche. I thought of Maria, who was naive yet sophisticated in her own sweet way. They were so graceful when they danced. And when they spoke, there was such precision to everything they said, their voices brisk and clipped.

As for the von Trapp boys, the ones most like myself, although they could be terrors, they were sophisticated in their liederhausen, nothing like my junior-high brother in scuffed Converse or John with his jeans and orange college sweatshirt. The von Trapps belonged. If they left Austria, it was only because they had no other choice. They left with dignity, songs on their lips. My family, by comparison, were interlopers, awkward foreigners bumbling into this old world not knowing which car was coach class or where to stow our bags or how to pronounce a single decent word of German.

The train shot over a highway, and I noticed a sign marking an exit ramp: "Ausfahrt."

I tried to pronounce that word in my mind and came up with "Ass-fart," which only made me feel like more of a yokel. Then we ripped by a tiny town, not stopping at the white marker announcing "Schloss Haus." It took me another minute to realize what I had just seen—two words that looked an awful lot like our supposed destination but slightly different.

I jumped from my seat and bounded to where my family sat.

"Did you see the station we just passed?" I hissed.

My father cocked his head, unable to hear. My mother shook her head, eyes widening.

"Schloss *Haus*, not *Klaus*."

In a panic, Mom pulled the map out of her purse and tore it open, looking for Salzburg then the surrounding villages. She let out a weary sigh, and I knew. I felt vindicated. Almost triumphant. They were so ridiculous, the whole lot of them. Captain von Trapp wouldn't be caught dead on a train going the wrong direction. Steely-eyed, firm-jawed, he had rescued his family from the Nazi trap. He had climbed every mountain and forded every stream, just so he could lead his family to their dream. But my own father? Here is where all that don't-worry, no-problem attitude got us.

I punished Dad with a scornful frown. I reached into the overhead rack and yanked down my flight bag. Now we would all have to stumble down the aisle with our suitcases, knowing that the Austrian passengers were laughing inside. Knowing that we had become jesters, in effect.

After we deboarded at the next train station, I separated myself by walking to the far end of the platform and standing alone, staring toward the tallest of the surrounding mountains. I glanced back only long enough to see that the others were scattered, too, letting my father humiliate himself with the station conductor, who kept pointing down the tracks then rolling his wrist to check his watch. The train back to Salzburg probably wouldn't come until dark. Hell, it probably wouldn't come until next week, I thought.

I sat down on the edge of the platform, letting my feet dangle. Then I stared at the mountains. What good was a trip to Europe if all you did was wander around looking stupid?

To my consternation, my father appeared beside me and eased himself into a squat.

"Next train isn't for an hour," he said. "We're going to get some ice cream. Want some?"

I didn't even turn my head.

"Hey," he said, "it could be worse. "What if you hadn't seen that sign? We'd still be on a train headed to Yugoslavia."

I refused to smile—to even acknowledge my father's presence. Not everything could be brushed aside with a joke.

"Okay, if you want to stay, you can, but I've got one minor problem," he added. "I haven't bought our return tickets. We weren't planning on having to buy a second set, and now it's too late to change money, so I'm afraid I'm going to have to use some of the schillings I gave you."

"C'mon, Dad," I blurted out, too outraged to stay silent anymore. "You said that money was mine."

"It's only temporary..."

"Unless we end up on the wrong train again and have to buy more tickets."

At this point, I locked eyes with my father, and I saw a change in the way he looked back. There was a flaring of the eyelids. He did not offer any comeback, just that stare, and under the laser-like heat of this gaze, I finally reached for my wallet.

"If you insist," I said.

Twenty minutes later, as I sat on the hard concrete, gazing toward the distant peaks, I began to feel alone. The long platform was empty. Not even the conductor could be seen.

And I felt hungry.

I thought about the money I had given back to my father and realized it had never been mine to start with.

I thought about how this might even be funny someday. It always was, in the end. With my dad, there always were stories like this. The camping trip when we forgot the poles for the tent. The road trip when we had five flats and stayed at a hotel that had hot water only if we flushed the toilet.

Although I chafed at the thought of my family already beginning to laugh about the situation, I couldn't help imagining how they would convert the incident into a joke:

"Remember the time we took the train to Schloss *Haus*?"

"Ja. Ja. Zat ist mien verst nightmare."

Why couldn't we have a story of everything being absolutely perfect, for once? Why always a disaster?

I remembered my father's piercing stare and regretted being so bitter. It occurred to me that I could not change my father any easier than he could change me. After all, I was the unhappy one who had decided to sit by myself on the end of a train platform.

When my junior high brother Nat finally came down the platform, nibbling on a dark sugarcone with pink-and-white ice cream, I didn't ignore him, as my first impulse told me to do. Instead I asked, "So was it good?"

"Yeah, man. Why didn't you come?"

I shook my head. "I don't know."

"You missed out. There was a guy with an accordion, and an old couple did the polka..."

"Sounds cool."

"Yeah, and you should have seen Mom and Dad. They even tried to dance."

I could imagine my parents spinning on the cobblestones, and all the Austrians stopping to smile. I could imagine people clapping along and my father kicking his legs higher, out to each side, as he whirled his wife around. Everyone would have been having fun there, in a circle around my whacky parents, and part of me wished I'd been there to witness it. Nat was probably right. I should have gone. And yet... how would I become my own man if I always followed someone else's lead?

Individuation 101

The man with the cross, wearing dark slacks and a wool suit jacket, leans into his burden. The trail rises, but he pulls the heavy timbers steadily, scraping the lagging wood over loose rocks. Centurions stroll alongside, indifferent, with skirts of leather straps and tightly laced sandals. Their swords swing like metronomes. The backs of their necks, under metal helmets, are streaked with dust.

A small crowd, all in suits and ties and modest skirts, follow thoughtfully, like old acquaintances halfway through a hike. It seems odd to me how well-dressed they are, and how formal in appearance. I think I can see one of my brothers near the front, but I don't push forward. I don't call out.

And so I started to dream, one Sunday night in the summer after my first year of college, drifting subconsciously into the dead of the night....

The morning before, I had gone back to my old

home church with my parents, stepping into the sanctuary and taking my place beside them on a pew halfway to the pulpit, where I got thumped on the back by family friends, glad to see me home. The high-paneled ceiling felt heavy, like the overturned keel of a ship. And the opaque globes of light hung like dim moons. I felt smothered, as if forced into a leaden vest. And after the sermon, when the congregation started to sing *Faith of our fathers, living still, in spite of dungeon, fire and sword...*, I stared in distress. These were people I liked. People I had known all my life. They were probably quite sincere. But suddenly I questioned if any of them were really thinking about the words they were singing. They seemed to me like mannequins clapping their mouths. I could not join in, even though I wanted to. My jaw clenched. My teeth hurt.

The man with the cross stumbles as the trail narrows into a cliff-side path so tight only one or two can walk abreast, stairstepping on the rocks. Far behind in the file, I can see him lurch, one hand hooked around the cross beam, the other reaching for balance. One of the centurions pulls a sword and hacks at the dragging cross. He slaps the blade, flat-sided, on the rump of the carrying man.

Strange, but isn't that my elder brother, lifting his hands to protest? Then my younger brother closing in to calm him?

At college up in Chicago I had been studying how people get "socialized"—inheriting a worldview from their mentors. I had learned that we are, to a great extent, a product of our environment. And I had begun to wonder what made me any different than the juvenile delinquent I met on a visit to a minimum-security prison. After all, if I had been born in that other boy's inner-city skin and if my father had done jail-time—if, in the absence of any father, the gang leaders had come recruiting—what would have kept me from joining and doing what all gang members do to protect their turf? What would have kept me from stabbing a kid from a rival gang and also ending up in prison?

For that matter, if that gang kid had been born here in Troy, Kansas, what would he be doing now? Preparing for a summer internship with the city newspaper across the river, in St. Joe? Sitting in the same church pew? Joining in with the assembled elders, all of them united with irrevocable solidarity: "Faith of our fathers..."

Even in the lowering dusk, I can tell that the cliff-face ahead is blank, no longer scored by the dark line of the trail. Where does it go? But then I come around a bend, and I see that the path slips into a shadowy cleft. The carrier of the cross has stopped. He turns in front of the dark entrance, looking back, and with a startling rush I realize it is my

own father, pale face sagging, jacket torn.

Alarmed, I leap into a half-jog, pushing around the others in their suit jackets and skirts. I call out—"Let him go." I shove through, even though the edge of the trail gives way on nothing, dropping hundreds and hundreds of feet.

Too late, though. The centurions prod my father into the dark, turning back to face the crowd. Then they usher my brothers through.

When I reach the front, what then? I become frightened by what might lie beyond—what might be required. Nevertheless, I push around the last few people and shout, "Let him go! That's my father!"

On the sidewalk, after the service that morning, I had stood alone for a while, able to hear the muffled chatter of the church folk back inside the tall wooden doors. It was quiet otherwise, out there on the edge of town—so quiet that I could hear the grasshoppers click as they leaped through the grass. The noonday light felt blinding, so I had to shade my eyes when I looked over the corn fields to the north. Rows and rows of uniform green, regular as corduroy. A blank blue sky. A little leak of tears at the corner of my eye.

In psychology class, the teacher had talked about identity crisis, saying that it always comes, one way or the other. Sometimes it can be put on moratorium, but it will always come. It has to come if the person is going to make proper progress.

She had talked to the class about the need to individuate. About the need to move on, hopefully toward intimacy with someone new and different. But she had said nothing about how it might feel in terms of old relations—here on the outside of the church door with the whole family inside talking happily to neighbors and friends.

The centurions, with thick shadowed faces, step together, barring the entrance. Their hands are on their sword hilts, breastplates dull and gray in the twilight.

"You are not allowed," they declare, holding me at bay as one or two other crowd members slip past, filing into the tunnel.

"But I'm his son!" I shout. And I push with all my might, risking that we might topple into the abyss.

"You are not allowed," they repeat, and their arms are rigid as steel.

Job Shadow

"Hey, tomorrow why don't you come visit work with me?" That was what my father said one evening after I returned from another year at college up in Chicago.

When I lowered my brows, perplexed, he took it further, "If you want to be a doctor, why not see what it's like?"

True, I was planning to go into medicine. However, this idea of a hands-on encounter seemed surprisingly unsettling. I resisted with a litany of excuses:

1. As a kid, I used to go to
your office all the time.

2. You mean you want me
to wake before 7:00?

3. C'mon, no one's gonna let me
wander around a hospital.

4. Dad, I don't want to look weird.

And my father had an answer for each of these challenges:

1. Five years ago I was working on my own, not at a hospital.

2. Getting up at 7:00 is part of being a doctor.

3. There are no police patrolling the hallways searching for doctor impersonators.

4. Look, no one's going to know or care.

Basically, I was afraid to do something so out of the ordinary, but I knew that my father knew I was afraid, so in the morning I rose grumpily, ate some shredded-wheat, and went out to the car. When we had reached the hospital, driving twenty minutes, I trailed Dad into an examining room, keeping my eyes to myself. Dad took a white lab coat from the back of the door and gave it to me so that I might pass as an assistant or medical student. Putting that coat on was like donning a costume for a play. Nervous as I was, I got a buzz from it, just as I had when I floured my hair to play Mark Twain in high school. Then I saw that the coat had a tag sewn onto it with my father's name and title.

"They're going to think I'm you," I said.

"I guess you'll have to give them your diagnosis."

"Dad!"

"Don't worry, I can explain if we need to."

In many ways, I was quite prepared to be in an examining room, given how many doctors we had in the family, including all three uncles and three cousins in the middle of medical residencies. I already spoke the language, since I had spent my childhood listening to my father and my three uncles swapping jokes about obstructed bowels and enemas, ignoring all the mock scoldings from my mother. It seemed almost natural to become a doctor. Not just natural—fated. And so I had always anticipated a moment like this—with me in a lab coat, wearing a stethoscope round my neck, getting ready to solve some medical mystery. Why, then, such nervousness?

I tightened up as the first patient came into the examining room; a college student like myself who had experienced a strange sensation in his chest during a summer class, as if something fluttered then caught. This peer was shiny in the face from perspiration, but otherwise healthy-looking. He just seemed pent-up, with his eyebrows knotted together.

After listening through a stethoscope, Dad sent the fellow to another room for an EKG, and when he came back, I was the only one to greet him because my father had stepped out to deliver records to a nurse. Despite the fact that we were clearly the same age and despite the fact that the patient had been told I was the doctor's son, he seemed to think I might have the necessary level of expertise. Either that or he was so worried he couldn't wait.

"So... what do you think?" he asked. "Do you wanna take a look?" And he held out the long slip of paper from the EKG.

I eyed the cryptic zigzag. "No. I think we better wait. I'm not the real doctor."

"Yeah, I guess so," said the young man, and he sat there awhile before becoming compelled to speak again. "It's weird, man, because sometimes I can feel something bumping in there, you know. It's like the damn thing has a busted fuse."

Now I felt like a complete imposter, desperate for my father to return. What if this guy had a heart attack while we sat talking?

"Hopefully the EKG will show what's going on," I said, and I excused myself for a minute—to go to the restroom and stand in front of the mirror, first with the lab coat on, then off, then back on. Buttoned up, the coat transformed me, covering my wrinkled jeans and the lettering on my T-shirt: "Kansas: It's not so bad." However, my black wavy bangs, cascading over my ears, were a clear giveaway—plus the small half-smile, turned up on one side as if the other side had refused to join. I was an obvious imposter, I thought.

A year ago, when I had returned to college as a sophomore, I had experienced a moment of vocational angst brought on by an advisor who said I needed to "declare" a major. Declaring seemed awfully decisive. It made me think of a founding father signing a political document.

Although I imagined myself a doctor, this demand for public commitment caused me to balk. I felt paralyzed. What if I picked wrong? What would the rest of my life look like if I was trapped in a never-ending hallway with patients behind every door pushing call buttons? To make matters worse, what would my dad think if I didn't follow through on what felt like an emerging family tradition?

Fortunately, on that particular day the advisor had been worn down by a long line of waffling students, and she said the declaration was not critical yet. Maybe I could wait. So that is what I had done, doodling my way through chemistry (which I found strangely abstract), enjoying biology a bit more because it was the study of things I could actually see and draw (like amoebas with their ectoplasm and pseudopods), but mainly thriving on the nine novels I was assigned to read in a study of "The Modern Novel."

Back in the examining room, Dad received a second patient: an old veterinarian with a possible gallstone. This man sat on one side of his butt, grimacing as if someone had pushed a nail into his flank. Next came a pasty-faced woman with a fever who kneaded her forehead. But the patient who had the most affect on me was a four-year-old who had fallen on a tent stake, striking her head so hard that it raised an angry abscess under a clump of crusted hair.

The abscess was as big as an egg, and the first thing that had to be done was to lance it, relieving the pressure. When the toddler saw the syringe for numbing the area, she howled and climbed her mother's chest, so Dad had to ask me to hold her head still. It was all very traumatic—the child squirming against the needle, the tears wetting the shoulder of the mother's blouse, the mother herself crying and trying to soothe her daughter, then the burst of warm pus that oozed onto the gauze I held.

Nor did it get any easier. When we went to the next stage, suturing the wound, my father made it clear that I really needed to keep the girl's head still. He threaded a hooked needle, and as he tugged it through the angry edge of the wound, pulling one lip toward the other, the child jerked and yanked.

I had to clamp her head more tightly, trapped between my palms. I fought the urge to run from the room and the girl's shrieks, and, as I held on desperately, I realized that being a doctor basically meant agreeing to confront pain on a day-to-day basis, taking on as much of it as the patients could carry. Suddenly that arrangement seemed much less appealing.

In the car on the way home, Dad wanted to know what I thought about my day of job-shadowing, and I became awkward. I hedged. "It was interesting," I said.

"I learned a lot."

"But what did you feel? You still like the whole idea?"

Forced at last, I said what I was afraid to say—what I had probably been afraid to say for a long time because it might bring disappointment. "Dad, to be honest, I'm not sure I'm cut out to be a doctor. I just don't know."

To my relief, he smiled. He was silent for a minute. Then he reached over and slapped my shoulder, saying, "You know my dad used to joke about me and my brothers becoming doctors. A farmer once asked him, 'So, Doc, you gotta be proud of these boys. I mean, how'd you do it? All four of 'em doctors?' And my dad just shook his head. You know what he answered?"

"Nope."

"'Lack of imagination.'"

The Rehearsal

I was working toward a master's degree in English when I began dating a young woman named Cathleen. Soon after, my closest friend from undergraduate years got married to another friend, and I was invited as a groomsman. I was just serious enough to bring Cathleen along, but as soon as we arrived for the rehearsal—back in the Chicago suburb where I had gone to college with the bride and groom—I feared I had made a huge mistake. One of the bride's aunts alarmed me by singing out, "Ahaaa, bringing a mystery guest to a wedding. I think I hear more wedding belllllls!"

Somehow I had not really thought that way—wasn't prepared to think that way. I just wanted my new girlfriend to meet past friends. So I became alarmed by the possibility I had signaled something more significant.

I had only seen Cathleen against another backdrop—as a grad student on the campus of the University of

Kansas. At K.U., she was a lively wire of a woman who shared a love of literature, having read some of my favorites. I was impressed that she knew about the rabble-rousing humorist G. K. Chesterton and that she laughed when I paraphrased him, saying we should all spend more time standing on our heads since it made the world new and interesting. I was also impressed that she planned to go to seminary and become an Episcopal priest. In fact, it blew my circuits to think of her—with dangly earrings, copper colored nails, and sexy leggings—standing at a pulpit.

Cathleen had red hair and she would nip my earlobes when we made out, which I found a turn-on. She also cared about what mattered in life—the big stuff, like what we believed and how we acted. Nonetheless, that night at the rehearsal dinner in Illinois, when I looked across the table at her, I started to have second thoughts. The father of the bride, who had been a Greek professor at my conservative Christian college and had written commentaries on the epistles of Apostle Paul, quizzed Cathleen about her supposed "call" to the ministry, asking, "Where in the Bible do you see any support for the ordination of women?"

My own father would never be so blunt, but I suspected he shared the same underlying skepticism, plus an unspoken concern about what would come of our relationship if Cathleen did not acknowledge the standard gender policy back at our home church—that the man should be the spiritual head of the family.

As Cathleen began her defense, with eyes flashing and voice rising, I suddenly saw her the way I thought my parents might see her, my mom included. I wondered if her long copper earrings were a bit too jangly, her voice too strident.

Actually, the two of us had already been wrestling through the whole ordination issue. That's because, fascinating as I found Cathleen, I had all the automatic views that went with a small-town Baptist upbringing. My parents' church didn't permit women to be ordained, so I had never seen one at the pulpit. Women couldn't teach except in Sunday School. As a result, Cathleen's interest in ordination had seemed suspect from the first. On the other hand, it had also seemed intriguing, and until now, it had seemed harmlessly theoretical—like a curious case study in a textbook.

Back at K.U., while philosophizing with friends who were Episcopalian, I had argued playfully from my Baptist background, and in the process I had begun to see the issue more from Cathleen's perspective, discovering holes in my logic. If I were to take her side right now, jumping into the debate with my former professor, I knew just how to start a strong counter argument. I would point to Paul's admonition for slaves to obey their masters, and I would ask if that meant slaves should never have been set free? Then I would ask: "If you are going to argue that we have learned, since that time, to move beyond a societal norm—slavery—then isn't it possible we have also moved beyond another societal norm: Paul's admonition for women to stay silent in church and to be obedient to male authority?"

I knew that's how I could help defend my girlfriend—if I had the guts to do it—but when she glanced across the table at me, I balked. Instead of helping out, I flushed and turned to the bride's younger brother, asking, "So what was your record in soccer this year?"

That night, after one of the bridesmaids had taken Cathleen to another house, I was shuttled to the house where I would stay. And when I fell asleep, I dreamed. I was out on an open plain walking with my older brother John, who had already gotten married. We came upon a rope ladder hanging in the middle of nowhere, going up over a hundred feet.

"Go for it," John said, so I took a shot. However, the higher I climbed, the more anxious I got. The crazy device was attached to nothing and swung in the wind. It bent in my hands, forcing me to climb at an angle. I missed a rung and clenched up. Even though I was now only ten feet from the little platform at the top of the ladder, I had no idea how I would get onto the platform or what would keep me from being blown off. Painstakingly, I made my way back down to the ground.

"C'mon," said my brother, frowning scornfully. "Let me show you how it's done." Then he leaped onto the ladder and climbed effortlessly, clambering up the wobbly rungs with the agility of a monkey. At the top, more than a hundred feet in the air, he hoisted himself onto the little platform then stood and pumped his fists. He shouted down to me, "Piece of cake, bro."

The next morning was the morning of the actual wedding, which meant that my groomsman's responsibilities kept me separate from Cathleen. I stood up front with the other groomsmen, and I carefully avoided meeting her gaze, afraid to turn my attention her direction right when my college friend stepped into a new relational dimension.

According to family legend, my father had missed his own wedding rehearsal, raising the possibility that he might jilt the bride. When he arrived, he explained that, while driving across the snowbound plains to her hometown, he had seen a hitchhiker hunched by the side of the road, and because of a wave of sympathy, he had not only picked him up but driven back thirty miles the wrong direction, delivering the half-frozen man to some relatives.

Not convinced by this excuse, one of Mother's uncles muttered that he would kill my father if he was ever unfaithful. But Mom accepted Dad's story quickly.

She sighed in a sweetly exasperated way, glad that he had done the right thing, the Christian thing. Soon he would be her spiritual head, and she was ready to trust him. With Cathleen, I couldn't imagine the same response. If I missed my own rehearsal, there would definitely be hell to pay, which made me more apprehensive as I thought about being here together in this setting.

After the service, when we went down to the reception in the church basement, I could tell that her patience was wearing thin. Although she had her arm linked with mine, chatting casually with other people, as soon as a lull came, she turned and pled with me, "What is the deal? You haven't looked me in the eye all day!"

I was completely stymied. How to explain the sort of things going through my mind?

Hey, I'm sorry. I find you really attractive, just as long as I am not sitting with people who think like my parents.

Hey, would you mind removing your nail polish and earrings and lowering your voice?

Nothing would work under the circumstances, so I just shook my head and said, "I'm sorry. It's hard to explain—at least right now. Can we talk later?"

Eventually, of course, all the necessary photos got taken and I put away my tuxedo. Then it was time to climb into a car with Cathleen and the couple that had driven us up from Kansas—another pair of my college friends, who had ended up at K.U. for graduate work. We left mid-afternoon, knowing we would arrive at two a.m.; and Cathleen and I sat in the back seat, separated by a big wooden goose that served as a planter—a bridesmaid's gift for the woman up front. Cathleen and I were silent except when the other couple drew us into conversation, asking about courses we were taking or the plans we had for life after grad school, which of course raised the whole women's ordination question again, not to mention another unspoken question: What about our future as a couple?

In the front of the car, our cheerful friends talked animatedly about their new apartment and their pet parakeet. They talked about the queen-size bed frame they had found at an antique store and about the camping trip they would take during the summer. They just kept talking about all the ways they were becoming more connected, while Cathleen and I sat silently on opposite sides of that hand-painted wooden goose, faces screened by a flowering hibiscus.

Ironically, we ended up running out of gas two miles from our destination, but that was an actual relief. The other guy and I walked the dark road for a gallon of gas, and by the time we returned, everyone was laughing with surreal exhaustion, joking about climbing a fence and tipping cows. I jumped out of the car as soon as we reached my apartment, saying, "Sleep well." Not until the next day, after a late service at the church where Cathleen was doing a pre-seminary internship, did I finally broach the subject that we had been avoiding.

I asked her to step out on the stone patio behind the church. "Look," I said. "I'm sorry about the whole weekend—the way I acted."

"Okay, but why were you such a jerk?"

"I don't know. It was weird. I just started seeing you how others might see you..."

"What others?"

"People like that professor. Or like..." I was afraid to say it, but I wanted to be completely honest... "like my parents."

She flinched, then stared into my eyes intently, weighing her options. It frightened me. "Hey," I said. "I shouldn't have done it. I like who you are. You make life new for me—and more free."

She kept staring, her eyes flaring slightly. Then she lifted her empty mug and smashed it on the patio stones. "So don't do that to me again!"

The amazing thing? That night, when we were on the couch at my apartment holding hands, she leaned over and nipped me on the ear. Soon we were enjoying the touch of each other, not afraid to be close or to look into each other's eyes. Somehow, even despite my weekend of waffling, we were together once more and happy.

Amazing, I thought, as she wrapped a leg over mine. I can tell this woman the hardest of truths, and somehow we get through.

First Dance

After we had said our vows and kissed in front of all those witnesses—such a host of accountability!—my bride and I were relieved to walk down the aisle and out of sight. We were relieved to ride to the reception alone in a limo then to eat little barbecued shish-ka-bobs, concentrating on keeping our fingers clean. But we became awkward as soon as the band leader called us forward for the "first dance."

How hard to have all those eyes trained on us. Cathleen gazed into my eyes. I smiled back. But I found myself wondering whether the smile was for her or all the watchers.

When I pulled her in close, trying not to step on her wide, expensive dress, I felt stiff. Her legs against mine made it hard to move more than a few inches. We toddled, turning slowly so that we might seem to be doing more than just putting weight on one foot then the other. Were we looking right, I wondered?

Our parents were invited to join us, and they came gliding onto the floor, each pair putting out a set of clasped hands like a prow. I looked to my father—large and graying—and I was amazed at how smoothly he swung his partner away and how easily he brought her home, sashaying. Away my mother spun and back again, chest to chest, legs finding space between legs. The two of them didn't just turn in place but swooped across the floor, following their joined hands as if they held a secret purpose.

Halfway through this long dance, I felt my bride's arms around my neck, pulling me closer. I heard her whisper, "I love you." I nuzzled her in return, whispering the same words while tipping from foot-to-foot. I meant it. I loved her. But I felt strangely frightened by the thought. My eyes were fixed on my parents' united movement—the way they had transformed into a single complex and graceful creature. When, I wondered, had they learned to dance like that?

Invasion of Privacy

While we were still living on the north side of Chicago near Cathleen's seminary, my parents came to visit and we gave up our bedroom, sleeping on the hide-a-bed in the living room, which was a bit of a romp since we kept rolling into the middle of the sagging mattress and finally decided to make the most of it. Cathleen was anxious about the squeaking springs. She covered my mouth with her hand. Then she padded into the bathroom and came back with a box of Kleenex, whispering how scandalous this all was, which only made it more clandestine and enjoyable.

The next morning, my mom took Cathleen to breakfast at a Swedish restaurant a few blocks away, and Dad and I stayed in the apartment eating scrambled eggs and toast and having a "one-on-one," as he liked to call it. Usually such an encounter involved reading a passage of scripture and discussing it, which was a practice I had begun to secretly resent, since I always felt a bit like I was going to a doctor for a check-up.

When I read the Bible these days, I was running into frustrating contradictions. Why was it, I wondered, that ministers in my parents' denomination didn't support the biblical passage about stoning rebellious children? If they were going to be so strict about keeping women silent, then why not stone kids too? And, by the way, where in the Bible were they instructed to put a flag up front near the pulpit? Or to pass an offering plate?

I didn't want to talk about such questions because that would cause needless tension with my father. I was basically prepared to squelch my true thoughts and to follow standard protocol. However, to my surprise the first thing Dad said, once we had finished our eggs and toast, was that he had a confession.

A confession? I had never, in my entire life, heard a confession from my father, which made me apprehensive. What could be so important to both of us that he had to share it? Had he cheated on Mom?

"Alright then, what are you needing to confess?"

"Last night..."—and now I was more alarmed because I feared that he had heard Cathleen and I making love, perhaps with some sordid twist I couldn't anticipate.

But no, Dad was struggling to admit something quite different. "Last night, instead of going to bed right away, I thought I would read, and I found a book on the night stand. It's a book I shouldn't have looked in, but I couldn't resist."

A book on the nightstand? Why was that so upsetting? I knew that our copy of *The Joy of Sex* was buried in the socks and underwear drawer.

"I don't get it. What made this particular book off-limits?"

"Because it was private."

With a kind of awful thunderclap, the truth hit me, and I sat there stunned.

"Are you telling me what I think? You read my journal?"

There was an almost imperceptible nod.

"How much?"

"A lot."

"Please, please tell me you didn't look at the whole thing."

Another slight nod and an anguished look.

"Are you serious? You just kept reading?"

"I couldn't help it. It was out there on the nightstand..."

"Just because it's out there doesn't... Oh c'mon Dad. What the hell."

My mind was leaping through the journal now, mentally flipping through entries.

The rant about my boss—an editor who had come back out of retirement to manage our division and who often talked to me like I was in high school.

The description of the new minister at my parents' church—as a self-righteous prick.

The reflection about Jesus getting more angry at people like that sanctimonious minister than anyone else.

The admission of struggling, even after marriage, with a desire to look at pictures of naked women.

The dream about following a woman into a hotel room only to have it turn out to be my mother and then to have the door beaten down by a masked man who, after being stabbed, turned out to be my father… .

I was sick now, like I could vomit. I was filled with a sense of doom. I was also very, very, very angry.

"Damn it, Dad!"

"I know."

"Well, then why did you open the book?"

"Because it was there."

"But you knew you shouldn't, so why?"

No reply was forthcoming, and in the silence, I remembered now that this sort of thing had happened once before—to my brother Nat in high school. Dad had gotten into his journal and read a bunch of entries then admitted it sheepishly, making Nat so upset that he had stayed in his bedroom for practically two full days.

Outraged, I cursed again, like I had never done in front of Dad. "Shit! Shit! Shit! Why do you do this stuff?"

Only then, at last, did my father lift his gaze from the floor and look into my eyes. Only then did he reply with a hint of defiance. "Because maybe it's the only way I'll know what's really happening in your life."

Just a Twinkle in His (Her?) Eye

When we had been married nearly four years, Cathleen once again forgot to take her birth control pill, and I once again got anxious, shying away from making love. But she said something she had never said before: "Well, would it be that bad if we *did* get pregnant?"

I was a bit stunned and gaped at her before shooting back, "Well, would it be that bad if we *didn't*?"

By this time, we were living in a suburb of Chicago, where she had taken a position as an assistant priest and we had moved into a small rent-free vicarage. We often went walking by a nearby school playground, and soon after that surprise conversation, we paused at the playground, where Cathleen started to ruminate out loud, asking what a child might look like if it came from the two of us. Red hair like hers? A crooked grin like mine? Freckles or no freckles?

One of her closest college friends had just given birth, naming the newborn Bernice or Brianna or some other sweet B— name, which inspired Cathleen to throw out several names of her own, but only male ones because she was positive—wasn't I?—that we would have a boy first. Maybe Brad, she proposed? What did I think of that? To which I replied that I was partial toward Bilbo. Or maybe Benito.

She laughed and punched me in the arm and we kept walking. But that evening as she was standing in the bathroom popping a birth control pill out of the numbered blister pack, she became quite pointed: "You know, I don't want to take these things forever. If we're going to have kids, I'd rather not be using a walker when it happens."

I tried to joke—"Hey, we can get one of those motorized wheel chairs. You'll run circles around them."

She scrunched her eyebrows. "I'm serious. I want you to be thinking about it, not just joking."

So, at last, there was no escaping the fact that she was ready to launch. The count-down had started. And basically, I was terrified. I hadn't told Cathleen, but I was afraid of being responsible for someone other than the two of us. I already found it hard to deal with another adult, let alone an infant. I had observed new parents, including both my brothers, swiveling their heads to keep an eye on a crawling baby or a toddling three-year-old. Conversing with them was like trying to converse with a basketball fan in a sports bar while all the TV's were tuned to the NCAA Championship Game.

To be honest, I had a rather-strong, selfish desire to keep Cathleen's attention for myself. I didn't want to get shouldered aside by a baby. Not at the dinner table when *I* was the one feeling hungry. Not at night when *I* was the one worrying or struggling to sleep.

But I wanted to be capable, too—and able to take what seemed like the next step in life. I had generally assumed that I would someday be a father, and it seemed "someday" had arrived. After all, I was past thirty! So the next afternoon when I got home from my commute to the publishing house and when I joined Cathleen in the kitchen to help with a salad, I said rather abruptly, "Hey, if you want to go off the pill, it's okay. I mean, I think I'm ready."

She was ecstatic, and she stayed that way for weeks, eagerly anticipating the magic moment. She was more interested in making love than ever, which was a nice benefit. However, to our shared surprise, she did not get pregnant right away. Six weeks turned into six months turned into a year, and she was still not pregnant. And though I was sort of relieved, I was also disappointed—and worried.

I had begun to look forward to the accomplishment of getting pregnant. It would be fun to announce the news. Cathleen and I would be joining the club, so to speak.

But what if we actually *couldn't* get pregnant? What if, in fact, I was the problem?

It's strange where my mind went. Suddenly, I began to wonder if God was punishing me. I mean, if ever there was something that seemed inspired by God, it was pregnancy. And if God was the One in charge, wasn't there a chance God was angry with me—self-absorbed skeptic that I was?

I began to wonder if maybe God was saying I didn't deserve to be a father, so it was quite a surprise when, after a year of "failing", one day I came home from work and Cathleen met me at the door beaming.

"I'm pregnant," she announced.

Suddenly all that waiting seemed worth it. In fact, the waiting even made the moment more wonderful. I was lifted on a wave of relief. Amazing. I was going to be a father!

Strange, though, how I became worried again after only a few months. Why was it that, on the way back from our first official Lamaze class, I found myself brooding in the rain-swept car, staring at the red tail lights that were reflected off the wet pavement and thinking, *Do I have this in me? Will I really have the strength and stamina?*

As if Cathleen could read my mind, she leaned over, and said, "Hey Mr. Quiet, I can't do this parenting thing by myself. It's a done deal. It's going to happen, and we're a team. Right?"

I nodded. Of course. But I had to push aside the thought of her alone with a newborn in her parents' guest room and me fleeing for Canada, to work as a forest ranger.

Frightened but trying not to be, I put my hand on her thigh and squeezed. "The dynamic duo," I said. "That's us, babe." And then it struck me that maybe parenting wasn't about being ready. Maybe no one could ever be ready for what was coming. They just had to be willing.

The Starter Dad

No, I wasn't ready. That became quite apparent in the delivery room, where the birth was basically a stripping away of power. I stood by helplessly as my wife did the true work, groaning her way into a private cell of concentration like an anchorite to her cave. I could only count between contractions, gripping her hand.

"Breathe in through the nose, out through the mouth," I counselled, mantra-like, watching her body assume its herculean pose, readying like a bow bent back until it must make that final Oh-God-I-can't-stop-now push.

And after? I was equally useless—while the baby, with wrinkled brow and closed eyes, bumped her leaking breast, opening its yearning mouth then turning spastic, droplets scattered on its cheeks.

As our newborn wailed, I asked, "Is he getting anything?"

"I think so," she replied. "Yeah, I think I felt something coming out."

But how could I be sure, being so uninvolved, unable to monitor what was or was not getting vacuumed out of her body?

Ten days, the obstetrician said. Then we'll have a check-up. However, when we got home to our house in the suburbs of Chicago, the little brick house next to St. Gregory's Church, the baby was always crying and Cathleen was always saying, "I hope he's getting something. I mean he must be. I'm practically spraying him."

"Enough," I said after six days. "We need to go see if everything's alright."

So we bundled the baby into the plastic car seat and drove through the frigid neighborhood, and when we arrived at the clinic, the doctor simply lifted a fold of infant skin.

After she released, that fold stayed raised and she frowned. "Possible failure to thrive," she announced.

Seeing our alarm, she back-pedaled. "I mean we can't know for sure, but there's no question this baby needs to go to the hospital. And I mean now!"

So that is how we found ourselves back in a hospital room with nurses coming and going. That is how we found ourselves trying to sleep on a recliner, reaching over to stroke our gaunt son around his IV-needled arm and giving him tiny sips of formula from a syringe.

We shared the room with the mournful mother of a baby who had a respirator tube in her nose and an IV needle in her scalp and a heart monitor always beeping. There was no matching man to stand by as the other mother shared her woes with Cathleen, no recognition of me either.

Fatherhood, I thought, as I stood and watched.

50 Ways to Hold a Baby

Because the breast feeding hadn't worked, our first child was now a formula baby. Conrad, we had named him, honoring my mother's maiden name. And Conrad was what any more-experienced parent would call "colicky."

This meant three things:

> After 7 or 8 pm, he was always squalling.
>
> 2 am was his favorite time to squall.
>
> Since Cathleen's breastmilk wasn't necessary and since she was practically catatonic at 2 am, I was the default middle-of-the-night child-care giver.

The baby monitor would alert me before any real crying began—when Conrad was simply rowing arms and making snuffling noises. This was a preliminary and could last a while. Nonetheless, I could not go back to sleep. The pauses frightened me, making me worry whether our recently-at-risk baby was still breathing, so I would listen for the next rustling noise, and though I could predict, down to the second, when the real crying would begin, this predictability made going back to sleep impossible.

I listened in a kind of suspended animation. 5, 4, 3, 2, 1, and the first whimper came forth in the staticky monitor like the mewing of a kitten. After a pause, I heard a more obvious distress call. And these complaints crescendoed, tugging me out of any remaining stupor—until I heard a tone that made it quite clear that sleep was now impossible. It was a shrill imperial cry full of indignation, as if to say, "Cut it out, I know I'm being listened to and ignored."

Groggy, I got up and staggered to the wall, reaching to steady myself. I slipped out of the room and shut the door softly, feeling for the light switch. When I hit it, the baby saw the change in the hallway and went into an even more intense fit, squawking from the nursery: "SOS. I'm in here. Somebody come ASAP. You gotta airlift me to safety—or at least to some warm baby formula and a rubber nipple. I know you are there. You better not be peeing. Not like last night. Oh, c'mon. You are peeing, aren't you!"

As soon as I had flushed the toilet and slapped my face with water, I quick-walked into the nursery to hoist our four-month-old out of his crib and swing him onto a shoulder. One handed, I got the formula out of the fridge and poured it into the bottle—right to the five-ounce mark. One handed, I screwed the nipple into place and put the bottle in the microwave and threw a tea towel onto my free shoulder. And even before I had gotten the bottle back out of the microwave, touching the nipple against my wrist to make sure the formula was not scalding, I already had swung the baby to my towel-covered shoulder as a way to signal: "Hey, chill out. No need to call the social worker."

Conrad was not convinced and kept crying until the nipple touched his lips, at which point he greedily latched on and began to suck. Sometimes it made me almost laugh. Sometimes, it made me almost cry.

While my son slurped, nestled in the crook of my arm, I rocked from side to side, staring at his wide open eyes, which were fixed on the air above him. And when finally he had satiated himself, I lifted him back to the tea-towel shoulder, waiting for the inevitable burp of warm, curdled formula, which would soak through the towel and smell yeasty like the inside of a milk carton. I used a corner of the cloth to wipe the dribble from his chin, and I kept rocking him on my damp shoulder, craning so that I could see him slip back into a satisfied state of near-sleep, his eyes fixed on nothing. Sometimes, I sang a bit to help him let go, making up lyrics:

You are sleepy, aren't you? I can tell.

You are ready to slip back into your shell.

Curl up now, and close your eyes.

Dream of how you'll grow up wise.

I found it very hard to be torn out of sleep like this, night after night. It made work hell some days, especially when I had to sit for hours in my cubicle, editing manuscripts. However, there was something strangely satisfying about being all alone at night with my son in the stillness of the house with the windows dark around us. There was something heartwarming about feeling him relax in my arms, slipping back to sleep. And something about rocking him even after the sleep took over.

Sunday mornings, though?

Ouch! There's no pussyfooting around that.

Cathleen was now in her third year as an assistant priest, which meant she had to get out the door at seven-thirty every Sunday morning to set up for an eight o'clock service. Even if I spent the 2 a.m. shift with the baby, I would still get the 6 a.m. shift—and on a day that most people considered a "day off."

While the rest of the world slept in and took long showers, I was on baby duty. It was just me and Conrad until the late service at 10:30 am, preparing formula instead of coffee, and playing with chewable toys instead of *The Chicago Tribune*.

I would talk to him, saying, "Hey, there, buddy. What are you thinking this morning? Did you notice the new leaves uncurling on our maple? Did you see the old man with the tiny rodent-dog on a leash? Is that a smile, or are you pooping?"

I would change his diaper, squeegeeing his bottom with a wet-wipe. Then I would pick out a church-going outfit, such as a white button-up onesie and some blue-striped seersucker pants with suspenders. I might put a blue beret on his head—just for style. And finally I would assemble all the necessary items in the diaper bag: diapers, wipes, a burp towel, a bottle of warm formula, a nookie to suck on, plus a plastic toy or two, just for gripping and shaking.

I grew frustrated if Conrad was being colicky on these Sunday mornings and could not get comfortable, crying about some impossible-to-define "need." However, when the two of us walked over to the church, I didn't feel as weird about my baby-care role as I had expected. It didn't hurt that all the women in the congregation loved seeing a father doing primary care. They all wanted to get a look, holding Conrad briefly and commenting on his snazzy tennis shoes or his beret. They all gushed about how cute he looked and how capable I seemed. And during the service, they cast side-long amused glances as I demonstrated an array of keep-the-baby-happy tricks.

One thing I had learned was that this child of ours needed a lot of physical change. Without that he was cranky. Keep him in one position, and the position would throw him into a fit. So I became adept at altering his perspective on the world, especially in public, where crying might disrupt everyone's well-being.

The "shoulder carry" was the classic starter. It allowed Conrad to look over my shoulder, enjoying whatever might be back there, including smiling parishioners who made secret little waving motions. It allowed him to look over all those faces if he chose, and to see the high stained-glass window above the church entrance, with its deep blues and scarlet. Or to stare at the organ pipes as they emitted their battery of sound.

A transfer to the other shoulder constituted another small change, worth at least two or three minutes of further satisfaction. But eventually I had to resort to more radical alterations, first turning Conrad to face forward, sitting on a bench made out of a forearm.

In this new position, he could look at the backs of peoples' heads instead of their faces. He could see all that hair—blonde and black and brown and striped with gray. And he could see the altar with its bright cover-cloth, where his mother stood in her chasuble, leading the call-and-response of the Eucharist: "The Lord be with you... Lift up your hearts..."

I worried that Conrad might recognize his mother's voice and get upset. I feared he might throw a fit. It didn't work like that, though. He just kicked his legs as if sitting on a dock. He jerked his arms and gurgled. And when he started to fuss, pushing back against my chest with his head, then I resorted to the next position: the cradle hold.

With Conrad on his back like this, staring up, I could make faces at him and finger wrestle. I could hand him the rubber key ring to chew on. Or let him suck at a bottle for a bit. Or put a nookie in his mouth.

Finally, then, when all other options had been exhausted, I went to the facedown cradle, rolling Conrad over so that he was draped over my forearm with one leg on each side and one arm on each side, his head nestled in my palm. This allowed him to stare down at the pew and at the floor, seeing all variety of shoes. It provided another hemisphere of reality that might entertain him a bit longer, especially if I transitioned into a two-step rocking motion, shifting weight back and forth so that he was swinging over it all.

Holding Conrad was a workout, that was what it was. And I took to it like I had taken to playing football in high school or lifting weights to stay in shape, trying to vary the lifts. I got pleasure out of the fact that my son, colicky though he was, did not disrupt the service. I felt more capable than in the first month of parenting. So I was proud at the end of the service, when Cathleen had gone down the aisle to the back of the church, where she called out, "Go in peace, to love and serve the Lord."

I called out with the rest, "Thanks be to God." And I made my way to the parish hall, ready to get some coffee and some more relief from women who wanted to hold

Conrad, telling me how remarkably quiet he had stayed during the service and just how much he looked like his dad.

What We Talked About

During a visit to my parents back in Kansas, I rested my six-month-old in the arms of my father, who leaned back in a recliner by the iron wood-stove and adjusted the sleeping infant to the center of his chest, head under chin. I gazed as Dad carefully arranged Conrad and looked down his nose at the sleeping face, fingering the boy's toes.

How strange it was to think of my father as "Grandpa." It was weird to put him next to my own grandpa—the tough surgeon with the bushy ears, the man who grew up on a North Dakota homestead and quoted Kipling and loved hunting and died of liver cancer when I was still in grade school. Thinking that way made me aware that Dad had once had a grandpa, too. I had never heard much about that man, aside from stock stories about his life in North Dakota, so I asked suddenly: "Hey, what was your granddad like?"

Dad lifted a brow, surprised. "There's not much to

tell you, since Grandpa died when I was three or four."

"Well, what *do* you remember?"

"He was a minister."

"*I know that*, but what was he like?"

"He must have had a backbone to tell North Dakotans they shouldn't drink."

"I know that, too. You've already told me about the bar owner putting whiskey kegs on his lawn to taunt him. But what about you? I'm curious what he was like for *you*!"

My dad—now a grandfather—had one baby foot in each hand, as if weighing them. He lowered his brow and concentrated. "Sometimes I got the feeling from Dad that Grandpa wasn't that successful as a minister. Maybe he wasn't cut out for it. More of a scholar. A classics professor originally...."

I nodded, feeling like we were finally getting somewhere.

"When Grandpa moved the family onto the farm, that was the first time my dad really felt happy. I think he didn't have anyone to remind him he was the 'preacher's kid.'"

"So was your granddad good at farming?"

"Probably not," Dad admitted. "I mean, eventually they moved back to Fargo and opened a boarding house."

Dad shook his head wistfully. "You know, I can only remember one thing. I sat on his lap. I'm pretty sure of that—because I remember putting fingers in his beard. He had a big beard with lots of white hairs.... Oh, yes, he also had a little game he tried to teach me. He had a small spring in his pocket, and he liked to push it down and release it, catching it in the air. He would release it and let me try to catch it."

Dad brightened suddenly. "You know, that spring reminds me of a story Dad used to tell. Apparently, one winter night in North Dakota, Grandpa was left at a rural train station by a member of the church he served. He had to wait a long time, and it was bitter cold. He was starting to worry because snow was falling.

"Anyway, he heard the train coming, and saw the light, and he realized it wasn't even slowing. Maybe the engineer couldn't see the station with all the snow. So... without really thinking, my granddad ripped off his coat and threw it at the window of the locomotive."

"Sounds like a crazy thing to do in the middle of a snowstorm in North Dakota."

"Exactly!" Dad replied, laughing, then peering down his bifocals at the sleeping baby. "I doubt he could have lasted an hour without a coat. It drops to thirty below up there. In fact, I've told you about Dad losing one of his toes in a blizzard, haven't I?"

I nodded and grinned patiently. "So you're telling me your grandfather almost killed himself by not thinking about potential consequences."

"No. What I'm saying is that he acted quickly. That

was what my dad liked so much. Because that coat flew right into the cab and hit the engineer."

"But what if he had missed? What if the coat got stuck on the train and disappeared into the night?"

My father peered downward as Conrad shifted his head, pursing his lips. Then he looked up and smiled softly: "Well, I guess we wouldn't be sitting here now, trying to decide what kind of a man he was."

Communion

After three years as an assistant priest in Chicago, Cathleen took a new clergy position, this time as a chaplain at the university in Manhattan, Kansas, the town I had visited so much as a child when we went to see my grandparents. Paradoxically, my mother and father had moved back to the area too, and they were beginning retirement in a log cabin on an acreage five miles to the north of town.

Due to my master's degree in English, I was able to get an adjunct position teaching composition at K-State, which helped to pay bills, and Cathleen took over with the small Episcopal congregation that had formed on campus. Since she was no longer an assistant, now she was fully in charge—which meant she trumped me in terms of spiritual authority. That was not much of a problem for me, but it was for my parents. Though they were smitten with their daughter-in-law, I could tell that they still felt I should be the spiritual head of the household. As a result, it was a big deal when, finally, they skipped their own service at the local Baptist Church and came to our Episcopal service.

As we sang through the opening worship songs, led by two students on guitars, Mom and Dad helped to entertain our two-year-old, taking turns sneaking him crayons between hymns or scratching his head. When it came time for the common prayers, they bowed along with the others, adding their voices to the mutual response: "Lord, hear our prayer." And after their daughter-in-law broke the communion wafer, announcing "Jesus said, 'Eat this, all of you,'" they surprised me by not just stepping into the aisle to let me out, but starting forward.

I came along behind them, carrying Conrad on my hip. I watched as they stepped to the communion rail looking like foreign passengers approaching a customs official. They seemed awfully sober kneeling at the rail. They did not meet the eye of Cathleen as she reached out to put wafers in their palms saying "The Body of Christ, the Bread of Heaven." However, they put those wafers into their mouths and chewed reverently. And when the deaconess came by with the chalice, they took it from her too.

While I waited for my own turn, I saw how supportive Mom and Dad were trying to be. I knew all the doctrinal barriers they had pushed aside: the distrust of rote prayers, the belief that bread and wine were symbols not supernatural sacraments, the fact that they never drank anything alcoholic, and, of course, the stumbling block of taking communion from someone who was not supposed to be ordained.

Gazing at them, I was filled with gratitude. I gave Cathleen a big smile as she arrived and put her hand on the head of our toddler, offering the standard child-blessing: "May God bless you in the name of the Father, the Son, and the Holy Spirit."

"And you also," said Conrad, who had learned to talk earlier than most infants and was now developing his own set of comedic comebacks. When he reached up with both hands to clamp his mother's hand to his crown, she was stuck, unable to move down the communion rail. Conrad held her captive for a full five seconds, reminding her that she was, after all, more his than anyone else's. Then he released, letting me pick him up and follow my parents down the aisle.

Back in the pew, our two-year-old pulled free again, eager to walk down the long wooden seat and whisper into the ear of his grandfather. He stepped into his grandpa's lap and stood there, facing forward, leaning into my dad's clasped hands like a sailor at a ship's prow. He stayed gazing out over the sea of parishioners until the communion hymn ended. Then everyone fell silent as Cathleen drank the remaining wine and folded a creamy napkin, placing it over the chalice.

The shared silence was palpable. The sanctuary was

absolutely quiet until, without warning, Conrad stood taller on his toes and shouted out one unexpected word: "HALLELUJAH!"

As might be expected, every face in the church swiveled, and all those faces lit up. But bold Conrad, already a veteran church-goer, did not shrink under their gaze. He did not grow alarmed or cower. Instead he stayed up on his tiptoes, leaning into the railing of his grandfather's surprised hands. Then he lifted his arms as if offering a blessing.

That child is mine, I thought, from where I watched. That boy, right there.

I could see some alarm in the eyes of my mom and dad, but I could also see delight. "Hallelujah," they seemed to be saying. In fact, the whole congregation seemed to agree: "Hallelujah, indeed!"

Climbing Lesson 2

Our breath turns to gray puffs as we begin walking down the snowy prairie trail.

Feeling a bit railroaded, I shiver in my coat and clap my gloved hands. I say to my sixty-five-year-old father, "Remind me, why we are hiking at eight in the morning on a day that is only twenty degrees?"

"Tradition. My dad always said... ."

"...I know. I know. 'If it's worth doing, it's worth doing difficult.'"

"Exactly. And it's true. Wait until you see the view. I used to come out here in high school and it was worth the hike every time. 'Top of the World,' we called it."

"Okay, but be honest. When your dad used to give you that line about difficulty, did you like it?"

"I hated it... ."

"So why are you still saying it?"

"Because I'm older and it makes sense. Think about it. If you cut a tree down with a chainsaw or cut it down the hard way, with a handsaw, which will be more satisfying? And if you break it down with a handsaw or a chainsaw, which will you enjoy more in the fireplace?"

"But if you use a chainsaw, you can spend half the day watching college football."

"...which won't be as interesting or memorable as going outdoors and doing something difficult. Honestly, what are you going to remember in a year? The bowl game or this hike?"

"Depends whether we survive..."

After another fifteen minutes of climbing, taking several gravelly switchbacks up the grassy hillside, we crown the top and stand on a small plateau, breathing heavily. The valley beyond is immense, with five miles of open prairie rolling toward the horizon. A river can be seen down there, with ice floes jamming the sharp bends. The cedars in the unlit crevices are ghostly with hoar frost.

"Like I said, 'Top of the World.' Used to be you couldn't see any of the town at all. A clean sweep. At night, not a single light."

"And what were you doing out here in the middle of the night?"

"Certain facts are not for public release."

"So did your father ever drag you up on this hill like you're doing to me?"

"Only once. I'd gotten my Eagle Scout badge, which was a big thing for him you know—that we boys all got the Eagle Scout. And for some reason he parked down at the road and wanted to hike up here on a winter afternoon. Seems odd now. He never hiked anywhere unless he had a reason."

"Are you telling me this is a 're-do'?"

"We'd have to have matches for that. It was so cold he actually suggested we start a fire and warm up, which wasn't his sort of thing. Too comfortable! The only problem is that we had only two matches in one of those flimsy books you get at a restaurant, so it had to be done right. I told him I could do it. I'd just gotten the Eagle badge, after all. Piece of cake. I gathered woody twigs from the brush—only the driest stuff. I pulled some cedar bark off a tree in the gully and shredded it up until I had a little nest. I slipped that into a tepee of twigs, and broke up some bigger sticks, ready to add. But the first match sputtered and my dad said, 'Maybe you should let me take a turn.' One thing I knew: A man's gotta stand on his own feet. So I said, 'No, I've got it. I can do this.' And I started the second match before he could stop me, slipping it down into the cedar bark, where it flared then snuffed out. A puff of smoke then nothing."

"Sounds like a fine and pleasant misery."

"Oh, you don't know the half of it. My father was not to be trifled with, and I had trifled. I don't think he said a word to me all the way back to the car—all the way back to town even. It was a very quiet, cold ride."

"So... are we going to try? We could rub sticks

together for bonus points."

"Not a chance. The sunshine will have to do. Nice, isn't it? How it lights up the grass."

"So Dad, why do you think Grandpa wanted to build that fire?"

"There's the million-dollar question. Same one I've been asking for fifty years. Why only two matches, too? And why did I feel like I had to prove anything, since I already had the badge?"

"Do you think he planned it?"

"No. Or maybe yes. I'm not sure he even realized what he was doing, but it was a test all the same."

"And if you could go back and do it over, what would you do? Light the second match?"

"You know, that's a tough nut. I guess I'd give the match to him and say, 'Sure, you try.' But then maybe I'd start walking back to the car while he did it."

"Just take off?"

"I don't know. Maybe I'd stay, instead, and see what happened. Or maybe I'd say, 'Dad, why's it always got to be so difficult?' Yeah, maybe I'd say that—and ask him 'Can we just let the fire go and enjoy being out here? Can we just, for a moment, quit trying to prove something?'"

My father and I turn away from the low morning sun and stand shoulder to shoulder, gazing out toward the grassy slopes that we have hiked and watching as the sun lights them up from the top, slowly inching down into the shadowed areas and turning everything, except the snow, a brassy yellow.

"Like fire," he finally says. "That's what I always think. Fire in the snow. Hey, thanks for coming up here. I know you weren't so sure. . . ."

"No, I'm glad we came. You're right, it's worth the work. In fact, I kind of wish we had brought your grandson."

Dad chuckles. "Now, that would have been a workout."

"True," I reply, "but you know what my father used to always say: 'If it's worth doing, it's worth doing difficult.'"

The Family Curse?

On a frigid January morning I was half-way through the drive to our child-care provider—two miles north of Manhattan, Kansas—when I glanced at three-year-old Conrad in the rearview mirror, bundled in the car seat. The car had not heated so he was hunched in his snowsuit, breathing little clouds of steam. Normally loquacious, he didn't say a word, stunned into silence by the 13 degrees Fahrenheit.

I didn't say anything either, as I crouched to see through the poorly cleared windshield. Outside town, I turned north, gunning uphill, but the car suddenly sputtered. It slumped, surged, then slumped again, and I realized what was happening.

"No, no, no, no," I moaned, as I checked the gas gauge. We were now a mile from the nearest filling station. With temperatures so low—genuine snot-freezing cold—I did *not* want to run out of gas.

After a quick glance in the mirror, I did a U-turn,

swinging the car onto the far shoulder. Maybe, if it was pointed down-hill, fuel would tip to the front of the tank and we could make it back to a station in town.

"C'mon," I muttered. But by the time I had completed this U-turn, the car was dead.

I whacked the steering wheel. I sat there with sun-lit frost blazing an arc across the top of the windshield. I didn't even try to turn the key, not wanting to know the result.

Then I heard it. An entirely unexpected proclamation from my forgotten toddler: "Damn."

And after a pause, a perfect follow up: "Right, Dad?"

I would laugh about this in the future. I would tell friends the story, and they would laugh. But each time I would also cringe.

As a child, I would never have said such a thing. The Bascom household in Troy, Kansas, had been a swear-free zone. Sure, I had experimented a little as I reached adolescence, letting slip an occasional "dang" or "heck," but even those words felt too close to real curses. Plus my father frowned if he overheard me, no doubt wondering, *Why would my son turn to words like that? I don't talk like that. My dad never talked like that. For that matter my grandpa never talked like that, being a minister in the Dakotas who was against everything unredeemed: fighting and drinking and, it goes without saying, swearing.*

Given my very reserved and polite upbringing, I had been quite shocked when, as a junior high boy, I had finally heard my father say the d-word. In fact, I had been doubly shocked because that curse word—which was uttered only once that I could remember—was said in reaction to me.

At the time, we were working on a little get-away shack a farmer let us build in his woods, down where an abandoned road met the creek. To build our hideout required carrying stacks of planks down a deserted roadway, weaving around saplings that had started to grow. I could be a whiner, prone to defeat, and all this lifting and weaving was definitely getting the best of me. To make matters worse, it was a steamy day with chiggers eating my ankles and sweat making my pant legs cling. Even my underwear seemed to be conspiring, rolling into clammy bands that stuck in the crevices.

As I stumbled through the brush with one end of the stacked planks on my shoulder, I complained to my father at the other end. "C'mon, Dad. It's too heavy. I can't go any further."

"Not far now. You can do it," came the reply, and I felt the planks continue to move forward.

I was much shorter than my father, and that meant he could not carry his end of the stack on a shoulder, where it would have been relatively easy. To keep the planks level, he had to cradle his end under an arm, clasping hands underneath. No doubt, the sharp edges were scraping his wrists and his fingers were screaming from gripping under all that weight. But he was insistent about continuing because, after all, we were so close now. We'd stopped enough. John and Nat had already dumped their load and were beginning to hammer.

"I need a break," I insisted, coming to a full stop, and Dad stood there slapping mosquitoes. To keep me moving, he pushed on the planks again.

"Dad, I can't."

"It's only thirty yards," he muttered, giving another exasperated push. This time, though, I tripped, having given up on all forward movement. And as I began to fall, I tossed the stack off my shoulder.

Here's the result: One end of the load hit the ground with a clap. Then a wave of weight traveled up the stack to where it was cradled under my dad's arm. The sudden yank ripped his fingers apart, and the planks snapped down, tearing across his wrists. They clattered on his thigh, springing loose. One even bounced back into his shin.

"Damn it!" he shouted.

And those two words, once they were out of his mouth, hung in the sweltering hollow of the old roadway, yellow and sulfurous and impossible to ignore.

That is what came to mind on that frigid Kansas morning twenty-five years later, when my toddler swore from the car seat behind me. Obviously, Conrad must have heard me swear before; otherwise, how could he know so perfectly when to use the word "damn"? It was fair game as far as he was concerned. Yet, how different his utterance than the curse Dad had spat out so long ago. "Damn," when voiced by a man who never swears, is like a lightning strike in one's front yard rather than a comedian's rimshot.

It was amazing how Dad's curse changed everything that afternoon nearly three decades earlier. What more could be said? I pulled the planks back into a stack. I shouldered my end and went down the road without halting. I knew my Bible, and I knew just what being damned meant. Though my father might have felt guilty about the uncharacteristic outburst, he did not apologize, and I never expected him to apologize. The curse actually seemed strangely warranted. I had been a wimp, and I knew better.

As for my three-year-old's premature, humorous use of the same word, it was evidence that no two fathers are quite the same. I could imagine my dad in the rearview mirror, frowning. I wasn't sure if my amusement was good or bad. I just knew, now, that I was not my own father and my child was not me and that everything about the next twenty or thirty years was going to be quite different as a result.

Behind Door Two

We had always thought that if we had one child, then we would have more. However, having leaped into parenthood, we were now less cavalier. After the trauma of nearly losing our first child and having to coax him to life by feeding him droplets from a syringe, my wife's dream of five children had come down to three. My own desire had been reduced to two kids—or maybe only one. After all, if we added a second, wouldn't that double the amount of energy required?

In the end, our firstborn was the one who made another child necessary. We would look at Conrad arranging blocks on the living room floor and think, he needs a companion, someone his size to play with; besides, if we don't go ahead with a second child, this one will always get ALL our attention, which can't be good, given how much attention we are giving him.

So Cathleen went off her birth control pills once more, which served as a reminder that, actually, we were not in charge. The first month gave way to another, then to a full year. And though we had hoped to keep the kids two or three years apart, my wife was still not pregnant when Conrad approached three.

We got anxious as the next few months passed. We talked about going to the doctor for fertility tests. Then, *voila*, Cathleen announced that she was "with child" and immediately, according to my old pattern, I began to worry.

After being in the hospital with Conrad, I was paranoid about getting ambushed by some unexpected difficulty. Would we have enough physical reserves to deal with another round of sleepless nights and diapers, feedings and doctor appointments? And how would we pay for it all? Not just the medical expenses, but all the added toys and soccer uniforms and music lessons and car licenses and eventually, the Mount Everest of all child-raising expenses—college tuition?

Cathleen was complaining of feeling tired—really tired. She was finding it hard to get up in the morning or to do anything. She looked pale. And when we went to the doctor for a check-up, he diagnosed her with gestational diabetes.

The doctor put her on supplements and told her exactly what to eat for the rest of her pregnancy. He told her she needed to rest a lot and be extra careful about not stressing herself. Which meant, of course, that we immediately began to stress about not getting stressed.

I was reminded again of how our first child had entered life—not able to latch on to Cathleen's breast, nearly withering away. Would this child be born struggling too?

Nevertheless, in all this storm of worry and preparation, Cathleen and I did not feel the need to know what gender our second child was going to be. Maybe we didn't want to know because we were trying to learn how to let go—to accept that we weren't in charge. In any case, when we went for the six-month ultrasound, we told the technician not to tell us which sex. We would let this child be a brand new gift, not unwrapped till the special date.

Yes, when I couldn't sleep at night, I still fretted over possible scenarios, trying to prepare myself. A girl might be good because that would introduce a whole new dimension for me—a kind of cross-cultural experience. On the other hand, a boy wouldn't need as many new toys, would he? And he might play with his brother more?

I was capable of over-thinking everything, but soon enough, the anticipated day arrived and Cathleen went into contractions, so we drove to the hospital and boom—another person entered the world. I was there for it all, standing by as the doctor cradled the tiny body out of my wife, and as the newborn uttered a good healthy wail. I was there as the baby was placed on her chest, still streaked with blood and placenta. I saw a penis, so I knew now what I was dealing with. A brother for Conrad.

I was also standing by, wincing, as the nurses cut the cord and banded it and gave the infant shots and put ointment in his eyes and stamped his foot with ink, making it quite clear that the calm warm environment of the last nine months was history. And I was there when Cathleen pulled back her robe, putting him to her breast.

What an amazing thing to watch this snuffling little creature, his eyes clamped shut, sensing the nipple at his lips and opening up. How wonderful to hear him cluck his tongue against his palate, ready to try, ready to latch on and pull the life-giving milk into his mouth. Nine months of waiting. Not a bit of practice. But here he was, going right to work!

When our new son clucked for more milk, sucking at the air, I was so happy I could practically sing. I went out into the hallway and started handing out candy cigars to whoever passed by. Blue cigars for a boy. Then pink ones because I had run out of blue.

"I'm a father," I told them all. "I'm a father again."

The Blessing

I know I should be more thankful on Thanksgiving Day, which only makes it worse.

Here we all are—my two brothers and their wives and a gaggle of offspring, together at the acreage where my parents are living during retirement—and all morning we have been having a fine time. My brothers and I have helped to burn scrub cedars in a bonfire. The young cousins have built a fort in a little stand of remnant cedars. The wives have reminisced as they peeled potatoes and boiled cranberries with sugar. And when my dad has blown a tremendous dinner call on his high-school baritone, we have all come running to gather around the orange rope-rug, quieting as he quoted a verse—"Jesus said, 'Let the little children come to me'."

Our kids grin now, as this playful grandfather asks, "You know who that includes, don't you?" And they laugh as he points to each one in a row—"you and you and you"—finishing with a finger tapping on the chest of our second son, Luke, who is riding his mother's hip, smiling angelically.

Everyone grins, including me, because I love my sons and love to see them loved. But inside I feel strangely uncomfortable. I look at the innocent, eager smiles of all these children and feel myself falling back in time—pressured to revert to well-worn customs, to become as compliant as they now seem.

This uneasiness spikes when my father says, "Now before we go to the table, we want to do something different. Just because your parents are grown up and have their own children doesn't mean they aren't still our children. Besides, we are all children in God's eyes. So we want to include them with a special blessing like parents used to give in Bible times."

The little cousins grin some more. This quirky grandfather is fun. So is this merry grandmother, who is wiping her hands on an apron, nodding.

I watch and know that my kids are lucky to have such bright, caring grandparents. I know I am lucky, too. Yet there is a part of me that can't accept this almost-perfect Currier-and-Ives picture of an American Thanksgiving—or my place in it. There is a part of me that has my own house and customs now, and feels unknown. A part that prays with the boys before bed but prays open-endedly, without requiring that they take a turn. A part that might sing a hymn to help them sleep but might also sing a John Denver tune like "You Fill Up My Senses" or might tell a story about Neanderthal boys having Neanderthal adventures.

This secret irritation makes me more irritable because I know I should welcome such a blessing rather than feeling as if I am being asked to do something tiresome or embarrassing. It's not like I have been forced to get up in front of everyone and move a pile of rocks in my underwear.

I try to relax as my older brother solemnly joins his wife in the designated chairs and as our parents place hands on their heads, calling all the other family members to step in and place hands on the couple or their kids, as if buttressing a tower. Dad prays for God's special dispensation, just like Abraham of old must have prayed, or Jacob with his twelve sons—one for each tribe of Israel. He prays long and hard, beseeching God to provide protection and to make the couple prosper. He prays for the young parents to have wisdom and strength and peace and direction and anything else that he might have missed by accident, such as repaired brakes and better tires on their car.

And this is where my mind goes as I listen: *I'm hungry, and now the game will start before we get done eating. I hope the Chiefs finally beat the Cowboys. Could I have played football in college—I mean if I had gone to a really small school? Will God strike me for thinking like this? Will I get an allergic reaction to the stuffing and have to go to the emergency ward?*

I feel guilty about drifting off like this, but I also feel that it is a bit odd my father is doing this sort of thing, as if he could time-warp back into the Old Testament. Maybe if this was the first time Dad had conducted such a ritual, then I would be more engaged. However, this is at least the third blessing, because I can remember him and Mom praying similarly back before any of us had kids and then when the first set of children were so young—still infants—that none of them remember.

The repetition itself is a problem. It suggests to me that Dad is concerned the blessing has not yet "taken" or that God still needs convincing. The repetition implies that he is reaching for something he can't quite touch. And this irritates me more. Is there a chance, I wonder, that my father is actually compensating for something he himself needs? Is there a chance that all of his attempts at blessing are driven by a sense that he was never blessed by his own father? That stern Doc K.F. died without basically saying that he was proud of his third son?

Suddenly, it is time for me and Cathleen to take our turn on the "blessing chairs," where my parents' hands settle heavily on my scalp. I feel a perverse desire to flick my head like a horse refusing the halter.

I have five-year-old Conrad in my lap, and Cathleen has his brother Luke, and I can feel all the little hands of nephews and nieces settling on my shoulders, trying to help create an effective spiritual connection. Although I am moved by their sweet virtue, I am also cranky enough to refuse to hold my wife's hand as brother John did with his wife. If honest, I want to break the circuit. I want to leap out of the forced circle, and I feel wretched for thinking like that.

So I submit quietly, gritting my teeth. And after we have repeated the ritual for my younger brother and his wife too, I have the oddest feeling. While the clan gathers around the table to ladle out mashed potatoes and sweet cranberry sauce and to put gravy onto the breast meat, I feel as if I am turning invisible. All through the long, loud meal—with the cacophony of food requests and jokes about Swedes and Norwegians—I have the sensation I may not even be there.

As I drive the car away that evening with Cathleen and the boys bantering, I am in the driver's seat, but I feel strangely absent. This is not the first occasion, unfortunately, but sometimes after we visit my parents' house, I come away like a magician's trick gone bad: Now you see me, now you don't.

Ronnock and Coolie

"Once there were two cave boys," I begin, and my sons smile from their pillows. "And these cave boys were not your average, dumb-as-rock cave boys. These were some of the brightest cave boys you could find back in 30,000 BC. IQ 60 or maybe even 70."

"What were their names?" asks seven-year-old Conrad, always alert at this hour, still thinking at a gallop.

"Their names..." I say, hesitating for a second, "were Ronnock and Coolie."

"Those aren't real names," says Conrad, with one blonde brow raised skeptically.

"Sure they are. Cave clan names. The sort that were easy to say if you only had grunts and growls and a few hard consonants to work with."

The boys grin, enjoying how I am making it seem normal to think about those ancient times as if they were yesterday.

"Now, these two boys lived in a top-of-the-line cave with the whole clan. They had ceilings high enough for standing and not whacking your head, and a living room the size of a movie theater—perfect for big fires and roasting mammoth and playing charades."

"Daaaad," says Conrad, "they didn't have charades!"

"Of course they did. They were always doing charades and trying to guess—saber-tooth tiger or warthog? Ostrich or giraffe? Cockroach or dung beetle?"

"I wanna know what happened," says three-year-old Luke, scrunching his innocent, rounded face.

"Well, no one had ever seen the back of this cave because in cave days you didn't go to the back of a cave. There were no lightbulbs to switch on, and sure, they might take a torch for a bit, just to see who chickened out, but all the legends said that every cave led into one huge cave, a cave that was actually the belly of a gigantic snake. Supposedly this snake would eat the world in the end, so you can see why exploring wasn't popular."

"But did they explore?" asks Luke.

"What would you guess? I mean these were high-IQ cave boys. They weren't the type to just accept stories about giant snakes. They weren't afraid either. I mean one time they had even shown the men in the clan how to catch a mammoth without anyone getting a concussion or breaking a bone, which of course was standard back then..."

"So they *did* explore?"

"Sure enough. Ronnock told his brother, 'The big snake's probably just one of those stories parents tell us to keep us out of trouble.' And Coolie said, 'Yeah, like that one about lightning looking for little boys to split in half.' The two even laughed a bit, remembering how they had snuck out in a thunderstorm after they had been told that kids who roamed in storms never came back. They both agreed that the whole lightning thing was bogus."

"They wouldn't say 'bogus'."

"Sure they would. They were bright kids, I'm telling you. They were already working on inventing English, so they had their own special ramped-up language that they spoke when no one else was around."

"Anyway, one night when the whole clan had fallen asleep around a roasted warthog and everyone was snoring in a pile, Ronnock and Coolie took two branches out of the fire and started back into the hidden part of the cave that no one had seen. They took extra unlit branches and put them down in their loincloths, just in case they would need to go further than expected. And they padded down the dark tunnel at the back of the cave, which twisted and went up-and-down and got more narrow in places and then wider.

"They found all sorts of amazing stuff. There were these horn-like rocks that hung from the ceiling. There were crystals the size of their heads, which had facets like diamonds and reflected their faces. There were other spikey crystals that grew long needles in a cluster like cactuses or yucca plants.

"And then they squeezed through a really thin passageway about as narrow as a bucket. The air coming out of that little hole was cold and damp, and Ronnock singed his hair when the torch blew back. He screamed, which made Coolie scream. And then the two of them both laughed because they were okay after all.

"A bit further and they came out in a room that was so big they couldn't see the other side with their torches. It had huge pillars and rock walls that looked like frozen waterfalls.

"This might be the belly of the big snake, they were both secretly thinking. And they were awfully quiet for a while, just staring around, but when nothing happened, they tiptoed forward onto a ledge and looked down, and what do you think they saw?"

"A dragon?" asks Luke.

"There weren't any real dragons," says his brother Conrad.

"Then what do you think they saw?"

"I don't know," says Conrad. "Maybe a huge hole that went down into the center of the earth and had lava in it?"

"Nope. It was a lake. Right there in the middle of the huge room was a lake. Which was great news, because do you have any idea what it took to get water where they lived?"

"Ten miles of hiking and climbing cliffs and shooing off crocodiles," says the smart-aleck oldest.

"Exactly! And they hadn't yet figured out how to bring any back with them to the cave except in a hollow log that weighed half a ton. So this discovery was like finding gold in your basement. Even better because you can't eat or drink gold.

"Ronnock and Coolie took turns then, leaning down over the ledge and drinking out of the pool, which had the coldest, most tasty water they had ever drunk, with not a bit of mud. They were so excited about their discovery that they wanted to go right back to tell the clan. In fact, after two big drinks each, they got up and turned around and started back toward the little tunnel, only they both fell over in fright and ran opposite directions. And here's why: There was a whole herd of animals stampeding right toward them—bison and antelope and a dozen woolly mammoths with their trunks up.

"I tell you, when Ronnock and Coolie saw that herd, they screamed for a full minute with their voices echoing all over that cavern and making it seem like there were fifteen boys instead of two. It took them another moment of complete quiet to realize that, in fact, the animals hadn't moved. They didn't hear any bellowing or thudding hooves. They didn't see any swinging horns. And when they looked closer, they both realized that this big crowd of animals wasn't real. They couldn't be real because they were flat, not round like animals in the wild. They were all flat and spread out across the wall of the cave around the little tunnel they had entered. And that's because they were paintings. Big, life-size paintings that looked just like leaping antelope and charging bison. In fact, Ronnock and Coolie realized there was even a cave man in there, running behind the herd with his spear, as if he hoped to get some meat.

"So... ," I add, "that's how Ronnock and Coolie discovered not only a water supply that would make life better for the whole clan but also cave painting."

"Wait a minute," says ever-alert Conrad. "How could there be any cave paintings if no one ever went into the back of caves?"

"Aha... Good question. I'm glad you're paying attention. You see this cave had been occupied by another clan a couple thousand years earlier, before the last ice age. It was just like our house, which used to be owned by other people and other people before them. And the group that lived in the cave way back then had different legends and had explored to the back and had developed cave paintings by using ashes and colored rocks like the red ones that had iron in them. In fact, the boys found some of the old ashes in a little bowl of rock, and some red crushed powder, and when they mixed that stuff with water, they learned how to make pictures on the walls too. But that's a whole 'nother story so you better go to bed now and try to figure it out in your dreams."

"Awww. C'mon, Dad," the two boys beg.

"Nope. That's enough for one night. You guys need your beauty sleep."

"We aren't beautiful," protests Luke, pouting in a way that makes him awfully adorable to look at, with his smooth, smooth cheeks and a sun-bleached cascade of hair.

"Okay, you need your smart-and-tough sleep."

And that is how I extract myself at last, kissing them each on the forehead. Then I creak up the basement steps. However, when I flick off the lights and gaze down into the darkened room, I am suddenly reminded of the bedtime stories my mother used to tell me when I was their age. Her stories always featured my brothers and me taking shrinking pills and riding on the backs of three friendly rabbits who carried us down into a fantastic cave of a different sort, a place called Candyland.

I grin, remembering how we begged for more. So this is how she felt.

What a strange phenomenon! To always be myself but, in some sense, my parents too. I can tell my own tales now, but those tales will be shaped by the tales my parents told, which were shaped by the tales of their parents and grandparents and great grandparents, going all the way back to Adam himself or to that ancient cave-dwelling genius who, one night, began to grunt in a new enthused way, determined to start the primal story we have all been telling ever since.

Climbing Lesson 3

We have gone only fifty yards up the trail. In fact, I can still see the car glimmering between the pines when Luke begins to complain. He sits down in the dirt. He's five, almost six. He's never been this close to a mountain, and certainly not from a let's-climb-it angle, with trees that march up the slope so thickly that there's nothing to be seen but red sappy branches and gray trunks like an impenetrable stockade fence.

I say, "C'mon, you'll feel better when you've hiked awhile. It takes time to get used to it."

Instead, he folds his arms and shakes his head, blonde hair whirling.

At that point, I pick him up and set him on his feet, saying, "Sorry guy, no choice. We're not turning around 'til we get somewhere."

"Hey," says Conrad. "It's not that hard. Look at me." And he begins a Groucho Marx demo, skinny knees bent, reaching out in long, long strides. He ascends ten yards with his face fixed in a stern British frown as if there's important business to be conducted, and suddenly, almost magically, young Luke is on his feet, laughing. He gallops after his brother, swinging a stick, which the older boy barely avoids by accelerating, getting twenty yards up the trail, then thirty, almost fifty before disaster strikes and down goes Luke, having stumbled on a rock.

By the time Cathleen and I reach him, he has teardrops glistening from his clamped-shut eyelids—little globes that shatter on his lashes. And when we pry his dirty hands from an injured knee, we find a raw patch clotted with dust. We wash it with drinking water, and I tell Luke I will carry him. I crouch down so that he can climb onto my back.

After doing an adjustment hop, I start up the trail again, trying not to think too much about my own sore left knee. There is no way I can do this for longer than a half mile, and I am discouraged. Why does everything have to be so difficult when it comes to a family outing? Last night it was the propane canisters for the camp stove, which I had forgotten and had to purchase in a town twenty miles from the campsite. Then it was my complaining wife, who got cold and couldn't sleep until I had brought a tarp from the car to place over her sleeping bag. And this morning it was Conrad, who fell into the creek right when we were leaving for the trailhead, forcing us to all go back to the tent while he changed into dry pants and socks.

I have had a bum knee for five years, ever since accidentally tearing ligaments during a workout. It functions fine as long as I don't attempt the same motion for too long or carry extra weight—like I'm doing now. Another quarter mile, that's all, I think, as I eye the ridge that will serve as my target.

Nimble as a goat, our nine-year-old dashes ahead, and I am surprised by his enthusiasm. Usually, he would be the one most likely to ask to quit, eager to get back to his friends and to "fun things" instead of family activities like this.

I am feeling the altitude, along with the pinching of something sharp in my knee joint. This is ridiculous, I decide at last. I didn't come out here to carry a fifty or sixty pound boy to the top of a mountain. Luke is young, yes, but perfectly capable of walking. So I stop a hundred yards before the ridge and squat down, saying, "Okay, bud, you've had a rest. It's time to start walking."

"Just a little more," he pleads, clinging around my neck so tightly that I have to pull his hands loose. Then, when I straighten, he slumps to the ground, sitting in the middle of the path as if he can't manage a single step.

"Maybe we should do a shorter hike," says Cathleen, and I groan inside. It's so predictable. The idea of a family hike—a genuine mountain-climbing hike—was something she had met with a tolerant smile, agreeing only because this part of the vacation was supposed to be my part to plan. I figure she's thinking the kids are too young to make it to the top and that she would rather be window-shopping at art galleries in town. I figure she is about to say...

"Honey, maybe the altitude is getting to him. He is only six, after all."

"If it's the altitude, then why was he racing around the tent last night, throwing pine cones? He's perfectly fine. He just needs to go a ways and he'll forget he fell down. Won't you, buddy?"

That final question, directed at Luke, is my attempt to sound jovial, but Luke isn't buying it. He stays seated in the dust, shaking his head. And now the whole situation has turned into such a stalemate that I consider just telling them all to go back without me. They don't want to hike? Fine. I'll do it myself. They can go shopping in town and come pick me up in the evening—or next week, for all I care. Maybe I'll just meet them at the other end of the range. They can figure out the camp stove and the sleeping bags and the wet tennis shoes, and I'll take my damn pocketknife and keep going!

"Hey, what if we pretend we're Pokemon?" asks Conrad, who has walked back from where he stopped hiking.

I almost blurt my first thought: *What in the hell? Why can't anything be real anymore?*

I am just inches away from breaking into a rant. I can

feel it on the tip of my tongue: *When I was a kid, I used to run and climb and dig. With my father, I tunneled into a hill, making a cave. I hiked all along the river bluffs, even in sweltering summer heat—not just playing make-believe games based on cards with strange-looking characters from a foreign la-la land.*

But even as I turn to give Conrad a wilting look, I hear our younger son reply, "Okay, but I get to be a Gengar."

Conrad scrutinizes his little brother for a second then says, "I guess. I'll be a Zapdos then, and we can defend the mountain against Fire Characters. You ready?"

So Luke rises to his feet and begins to walk, telling his brother what strengths he has and how he wants to use them. Then the two of them begin to jog in response to imagined threats, swinging their arms as if repelling blows and sending out enchanted blasts of energy. They rise up the mountain in tandem, with the older boy choreographing each scene and calling through the trees, "Watch out. They're behind you. Stay in the shade. Levitate now. You can shadow-tag then I'll hit them with a lightning bolt. Do it, do it, do it. Okay, let's get out of here."

I marvel. I cannot believe the ingenuity of Conrad. Nor the sheer kindness—the way he has skillfully stepped in to help.

When my wife reaches for my hand, I frown for a

second. She is smiling as if savoring an inside joke, and I want to pull away. But, instead, I let go of my natural inclination to resist. I let myself enjoy this moment of unexpected relief, walking hand-in-hand, murmuring amused commentary about the galloping boys and the imagined adventure that is taking them up the steep, rocky slope, closer to my hoped-for goal: a lake at timberline.

When at last the two boys lag, asking for lunch, I tell them just a little further. I ask what character *I* can play—"Maybe an Onix?" Then I begin to employ my own special strength—super-fast tunneling—to clear a way up the mountain, pouncing out of secret underground corridors and sending foes flying with slashes of my iron tail. I thunder up the forested trail, throwing rockslides to each side, my headblade slicing a ravine. "Come on!" I yell. "They can't hit you inside the trench!" And when an unexpected Charizard ambushes me from the air, flattening me with a Heat Wave, my two sons come to my rescue, zapping the Charizard right out of the sky and leaving it trapped by a Poltergeist.

Off we go again, ascending further up the mountain with our unique powers. And Cathleen comes close behind, jogging and cawing, having transformed into a leather-winged Aerodactyl that can divebomb enemies, stunning them with Supersonic Blasts. We are all so invested in this make-believe scenario that we are equally surprised when, suddenly, the trees fall away and we find ourselves standing in an immense bowl above timberline with ragged teeth-like peaks above, and huge fields of fallen stone. Swathes of snow streak the valley walls, secreting streamlets of icy water. And there, right in front of us, is a whole lake, sparkling in the breeze, black in its depths and emerald along the shore.

"Guys," I say. "There is something we've got to do. Even before we eat, we've got to do this." And I step toward the lake, peeling off my jacket and shirt.

"No way!" yells Conrad. "We'll freeze."

"Yeah! And that's the fun of it," I reply, sitting down to remove my shoes and socks. "How many guys do you know who can say they went swimming in a lake that is pure melted snow?"

After I have pulled off my pants and stand there in nothing but underpants and goose pimples, Luke begins to giggle, sitting down on a rock to untie his shoes. Then his bigger brother begins to unzip his jacket, murmuring, "This is nuts!"

Cathleen calls out, "Wait a minute. I've got to get a picture!" But before she can fish the camera from her pack, we are out there in the bone-chilling water, balancing on slippery rocks. And before we lose our collective nerve, we hunch our shoulders, count to three, and plunge down, disappearing into the arctic liquid.

When we heave into the air, our shouts reverberate against the cliffs, making the whole valley tremble.

For an instant we are utterly here in the quiddity of what we have done: completely alive, completely alert, completely aware of the amazing realm that encircles us.

I lift my arms and yodel as my wife clicks the camera. The boys flex their stringy biceps, teeth chattering, blonde hair plastered to their frigid skulls. She laughs as they ham it up in the buff. Then the three of us come wallowing out of the lake and scrabble toward our loose clothing, alarmed by approaching voices. Quickly, we hopscotch to a shielding boulder, where we drop down and wrestle into pants, pulling them over clammy skin and wet undershorts. And when the next group of hikers steps into the clearing with awed gazes, we emerge from behind the boulder, hair awry, smiling smugly because, despite Luke's reluctance and Cathleen's hesitations and my own self-centered grouchiness, we have accomplished something quite special. With the help of Conrad's precocious imagination, we have not only made it to this high beautiful valley, but we have created our own family legend.

How Fast He Ran

I am grumpy once more. That's because even on this day, a Saturday, I didn't get to sleep in. Instead, Luke, now eight-years-old, had to be suited up in sweats and cleats then delivered to the YMCA playing fields.

It is a cold October morning here in the town of Newton, Iowa, where we have lived since Cathleen became the rector at the local Episcopal church and I got a job at the area community college. There is a light layer of frost silvering the grass, and I feel extra irritable when I realize I forgot to bring a hat or gloves. While Cathleen drifts down the sidelines to talk with members of the church, I stand alone, shoulders hunched, hands in pockets. Even as Luke comes onto the field after the kickoff, I am grumbling internally, wondering if the halves will take twenty minutes or thirty.

These days, I feel that all I do is serve as a shuttle driver, getting the boys to school then off, across town, to piano lessons or drama practice or soccer or sleepovers. I protested when Luke begged to join friends in a new flag-football league. I tried to talk him out of adding another activity. Then I wearily drove him across town to sign up.

Twice a week now I drop everything at 3:30 p.m. I leave my office at the college to drive Luke to practice at the YMCA. Then I sit in the car for over an hour, struggling to concentrate on the homework sheets I need to grade. I know that Cathleen would do more shuttling if she could. I also know that I shouldn't expect her to do it, as so many women have felt pressured to do. I'm okay being this involved... except when it seems unrelentingly constant.

Distracted by such thoughts, it takes me a moment to actually realize, during the first play of the game, who has rolled out to the right as if preparing to pass—my eight-year-old son!

I wonder whether Luke has the necessary arm, and whether the kids are old enough to really catch a pass. However, instead of throwing the ball, he hands it off quite deftly to a wide receiver who is scampering back the opposite direction, completing a reverse that is a complete surprise—not just to the opposing team (which has, as a whole unit, gone chasing after the quarterback), but to the parents on the sidelines, who begin cheering wildly or groaning.

The galloping receiver shoots toward my sideline completely alone, then turns and runs the full length of the field, getting into the end-zone uncontested. "Great play!" I shout, almost forgetting for a moment how frustrated I have been.

A kickoff follows and a few more plays. Then the ball gets punted back to Luke's team, and this time I watch more attentively, no longer counting minutes until everyone has to be packed up and shuttled home. On the first play, Luke rolls to the right again as if planning to pass. The wide receiver comes dashing toward him like before, and Luke hands off.

"No, not the same play," I almost shout. But instead of running for the sideline, the receiver suddenly stops, plants, and throws a pass back the way he came.

To whom? I wonder, not realizing that my own son has continued running out there, curling downfield.

When I *do* realize what is happening, I think, *Oh Lord, please let him catch it.*

The throw is wobbly and a bit short, and Luke has to slow down, reaching back. He bobbles the ball a bit but gets it wrapped up in his arms eventually. He side-steps the only defender who has remembered to stay wide. The rest of the opposing team are locked on the reversing wing, not wanting to get outrun again, and by the time they realize this repeat-reverse is a ruse, they are all moving the wrong direction.

"Go, go, go!" I shout, forgetting all grumpiness.

What a marvel to see my son throw his head back and gallop, making a wide bend down the far sideline, the ball a bit too big under his arm, like an over-stuffed pillow. What a marvel to see him, only eight-years-old, sprint so hard and fast, dodging one more kid and blazing toward the place where he will either get cut off or make it through.

The opposing team turns now, as a complete herd, and stampedes back at a diagonal, hoping to intercept their opponent, so it is a double delight to see Luke suddenly brake and pivot, coming right back across the field on a completely new arc. The defenders aren't prepared for that either. Once more, they are too committed. As Luke turns down the sideline, he is not about to get cut off, not even by the fastest boy on the other team, who makes a desperate lunge and rolls out of bounds.

Our son takes two last strides and dives across the goal line with the ball out in front of him like a scene straight from the NFL. It is all very impressive, and I shout along with all the other parents, enjoying the zaniness of this fake reverse and my son's unexpected switchback. I am proud, sure, but what I feel more fundamentally is the sheer delight of seeing Luke move so fast. I had no idea he could accelerate like that—as if he had found some other gear inside himself. It is such a happy sort of running—full of hope and possibility—that I realize my throat aches. My eyes have gone wet, and I wipe them before anyone might notice.

Later, when Luke gets into the car with his cheeks

red from the cold, I clap him on the back and tell him, "Buddy, great game. You were really moving out there." All the way back to the house, I do not think about the fact that I am once again shuttling one of the boys from an activity or that it is a Saturday and I could have stayed in bed. As I drive, I am almost eager to see the next game.

Climbing Lesson 4

The cliff isn't hardly a cliff. More of a tall outcrop. But when I begin to hoist myself up the cracked face, reaching for handholds, Conrad, now in junior high, cautions loudly, "Not smart, Dad."

The way he speaks, barely concealing his anxiety, makes me more determined. I take a big climbing step, lifting myself onto a ledge.

"Seriously, Dad!"

I take another step onto another smaller ledge.

"C'mon, what are you trying to prove?"

I sigh, wondering when my thirteen-year-old began to talk like a therapist. The boy's question makes me remember what my actual therapist asked not long ago, "So why do you think you see yourself as 'old' all of a sudden?"

"You worry too much," I call out to Conrad, standing ten feet up the rock face. "Let me show you how it's done."

Maybe it is those words slipping out of my mouth which make me tingle with déjà vu. As I lift my leg again, testing a fist-shaped protrusion with my boot, I feel I have been here before. I cannot recall the occasion, but I recognize an echo of something already said.

The next foothold seems awfully small and I will have to lunge, but if I wait any longer, I will recall what is reverberating in me. I will recall the moment when my own father—top-heavy and cocky—stood high above me in a tree, determined to show he could go higher.

I don't wait. Like a salmon rising to the falls, I leap, reaching for a small, overhead lip—

My toe catches and holds long enough for me to grab the lip of rock. Then my foot slips loose and I find myself hanging by four fingers, face scraping limestone. I cling there, swinging legs blindly, feeling my breath bounce off the rock, until finally a toe finds a tiny purchase and I am able to put some weight onto it, to get my other hand onto the lip above, and to pull myself to safety.

It is not until I turn around to look down, saying "See, that wasn't so bad," that the past comes tumbling back. Maybe it is the paleness of my son's face that causes the memories—how alarmed I felt as I raced to my own fallen father and how the man just lay there on his back, unable to breathe, all bravado knocked loose. Also, how I was forced to consider, for a terrifying moment, what it would be like to have no father at all.

Still, I smile as I look down at Conrad—trying to make light of the moment, trying to brush away any thought of what could have happened.

He is completely silent, looking up in clenched alarm. Then he screams as hard as he can, his neck muscles straining—"IT'S NOT FUNNY, DAD!"

I stop smiling. I look down in a softer way and admit, "I know. It's pretty stupid really." But even as I make this concession, I wonder what Conrad will remember in another thirty years. Will he, by then, be inclined to make his own climb, determined to get higher? And will he look down just like this? Will he look at his own son and think, *My God, this is just what Dad must have felt*!

The Roadie's POV

There are five teens on our screened-in back porch, practicing as a band. Because of that, I can't hear a thing the football commentators are saying as I try to watch my favorite college team (Kansas State University) play against my least favorite (Oklahoma). Now I know why high school bands are "garage bands," not "back-porch bands." The cumulative sound assaults my eardrums—the shriek of the lead guitar, the bumpy "ba-dump" of the bass, the thump and clatter of drums. I even feel the music in my butt, where the couch shudders.

When I look to the window between me and them, I can see the glass pulse. Then I look through, and it is as if I am watching the boys on TV, instead of the football game. Each band member is engrossed in his own part of the song. The bass player, usually reticent and non-demonstrative, arches back then bows over his strings, eyes hidden by a screen of hair. The keyboardist, a polite kid from an East Indian family, flicks a shiny black mop out of his eyes and stabs his way through a set of chords, elegant fingers jabbing at the keys. And our son Luke, three years younger than any of them, paradiddles with his eyes up, watching to make sure he is in time before he flicks a wrist for a cymbal crash.

Our son Conrad is leader of the band—the one who writes the songs and tends to play lead guitar. And right now, he is grimacing into a microphone, calling out an anguished refrain. For a moment, he has the naked look of someone in intense pain, face crunched, eyes closed as if he is trying to pull a nail out of his hand. He is completely gone, ensconced in the aural realm of his song. He sings as if no one else exists, as if it will take all his might to be heard from there in the expressive vortex of his own words.

In an hour I will become a roadie for this band, as I have done a dozen times. I will help to schlep drums and amps and microphone stands to the station wagon, arranging them so that they don't topple into each other. I will drive forty minutes into downtown Des Moines and help to carry all the stuff up a flight of stairs to the concert venue where teen bands from all over the state are going to compete for a chance to perform at this summer's annual outdoor rock festival.

I don't know yet that my sons will win the contest and get their moment on the main stage. I don't know that I will get to see them up there like a professional rock-'n-roll band, each of them projected to five times their size on a jumbotron. Or that Conrad will climb the scaffolding on the side of the stage, singing from twelve feet up, then come down and dive into the audience, crowd surfing with the mic to his lips. But when I sit here in the den of the house, watching the band, I feel the loveliness of this particular moment. They are loud, yes, but they are quite good, and I am glad to be a father who allows them to practice at his house.

I nod to the rhythm and savor their solo riffs. I thrill at the words when I can make them out. Conrad is a poet really, coming up with surprisingly innovative lyrics, not just the standard one-line zingers that get repeated by a lot of bands. And Luke is a precocious drummer, setting the tempo for the whole group even though he is so much younger than the rest.

I remember when this band was forming. Conrad would bring his buddies over to jam on the back porch, but they were frustrated because there was no drummer and the only one available was someone none of them liked. Then the guys realized that Luke, still in junior high, was actually a drummer, and they convinced Conrad to let his little brother take a shot: "What can it hurt? Why not let him at least practice with us?" Thus Luke became, perhaps, the youngest musician in all the local bands, and the two brothers began a new dimension in their relationship.

That's what strikes me now—that both of my sons

are out there together, bonding. Luke glances to Conrad, waiting for a cue to close off the song, and I realize that they are learning a language that will be theirs alone, a language that will last the rest of their lives.

I don't know what will come of the concert tonight. I just know that when I watch my sons on the porch, even though I have been pulled away from the football game, I am grateful. It is a pure delight to see the two guys being creative together and doing it well. They do not need song sheets the way I needed printed music when playing trumpet in high school. They play extemporaneously and organically, feeling their way into what is possible. They listen to each other and to the communal sound that is forming, and they give themselves over to it.

When they take the stage tonight, I know that they will not balk at being in front of so many people, including other bands. They will light up and let themselves burn, flaring brighter on the stage, unafraid of honest words about love and loss and social ills and personal demons.

Who cares whether they win the "Battle of the Bands." Who really cares? I am just happy to see them rehearsing their honest selves—hopefully helping others to be as honest and free.

When Nothing Else Matters

When Conrad throws open the bedroom door at 3 a.m., letting it clap against the wall like a door kicked down in a crime drama, I rise up in bed startled, ready to leap for the ceiling and hang there. Cathleen is clenched to my arm crying out, "What's wrong? What's wrong?" But our eighteen-year-old responds with unexpected bliss, as if he has hardly heard her and needs to complete some sort of ecstatic monologue that began long ago: "Mom, Dad, it's okay. Everything's okay. Really you don't need to worry. I've got it figured out..."

Here he is, our gangly high school graduate still in jeans and T-shirt, thunderclapped into our dreams as if he is a sent prophet, a whirling dervish of divine revelation, Shiva himself bringing us the great revelation.

Conrad crawls into the bedspread ditch between us and puts his arms around our shoulders. He laughs a little. He is Lennon and Oko Ono rolled into one—full of a transcendental love that has to be shared right now, not a minute later. "Nothing matters. It just doesn't. So everything's gonna be better."

Finally I begin to think, asking the first question that comes to mind: "Bud, what have you been drinking?" That's what I ask, although I am wondering if, in fact, the boy has been snorting or puffing or needling or something more creative that I don't know about.

"That doesn't matter," Conrad says. "Don't you see? It's not about that."

"Well, it's about that for me," says Cathleen, "especially at 3 a.m. wakened by a son who can't stop talking."

"You don't have to worry about me, though. That's the point. I've got it figured out."

"But did you take something to figure it out?" I ask.

A big sigh. "It doesn't matter, Dad. It's harmless."

Despite Conrad's irrepressible enthusiasm, I feel very strongly that being instructed about the deep truths of existence at 3:00 a.m. on a random morning is not pleasant. This night my body has sunk into desperately needed rest, savoring the complete abandon of floating on the dark depths of sleep, and now I have been yanked into strobe-light alarm.

I want to scream. Instead, I speak quietly and calmly. "What exactly did you take?"

"Mushrooms. That's all."

"You did what?" Cathleen yelps. "When? How much?" And I begin thinking, How can my son—MY son—be telling me this? I never did anything like this. Psychedelics? What else, then, has he tried? And how did it get to this point without us knowing? Is it because we've always been too lax, letting him go play with that damn band at the bars that allow teens to perform? Is it because we have taken him down there ourselves and hung out, acting like we didn't notice that half of the bands had to go into the alleyway to smoke weed or that they had names like Poison Control Center?

"Dad, I love you," Conrad suddenly says. "That's the real deal. I just want you to know. Nothing else matters really. And you, too, Mom."

Even as I hear my son saying this very important thing, I am leaping past it, full of fist-clenching frustration. If you loved me, I want to say, then you would not be bursting into my bedroom at three in the morning, tripping on mushrooms. If you loved me, then you would be going to bed at eleven like a normal healthy youth, and sleeping in just a bit, until nine in the morning. let's say, instead of two in the afternoon.

"I love you too," I say into the shadows, "But I'm tired, guy. And I've got to get up and lead a class in the morning. So we may have to talk about this another time."

"Yeah, no problem. I wanna talk anyways. Let's talk more. We need to talk."

He stays right there in the rut between us, and his breathing gets more steady after a bit, and when I wake to the alarm three hours later, he is still asleep in the middle of our bed, his angular features softened and turned innocent by the blue-gray light.

Yes, I think as I slip from under the blankets, let's talk. We need to talk more.

Paternity Test

I am in my office at the community college taking a badly needed break, when the secretary from down in academic affairs knocks and says, "Sorry to bring bad news..."

I am prepared to hear that one of my colleagues is sick and I need to cover an extra class. Or that a student just backed into my car in the parking lot. I am *not* prepared to hear, "I'm afraid your dad has had an accident. They think he broke his hip."

Six hours later, I am in a surgical waiting room in Kansas. My weary, half-smiling, half-grimacing mother is there too, surrounded by sympathetic well-wishers, and I am forced to receive the whole story from these nodding well-wishers, conscious that they know more than I do—that I am late in the crisis-control department.

Since it's March, they explain to me, all the farmers have been in the pastures clearing brush. Your dad decided to join several men working on the backside of the neighbor's pasture, clearing away some of the smaller invading cedars. There was frost out there, they explain, but a lot of it had melted by the time your dad drove his pickup into the pasture. Anyway, he was late, so the others had moved down into the trees...

As I listen, I imagine my almost eighty-year-old dad gunning his way up the rutted driveway into the pasture, fishtailing just a bit too much. I know that he was probably enthusiastic when he got up there on the hilltop, glad for the bracing breeze and the strength to still handle a bow saw. I imagine him facing into the cold wind and taking a big gulp of it, right down to the bottom of his lungs. What, then, went wrong?

Too bad your dad got there late, the well-wishers say. But since he was not sure which direction the other men went, he had to start off on his own, straight down the far hillside.

That slope faces north, they remind me. It hadn't thawed yet, and apparently that's why his feet went out from under him... .

Finally, my mom chips in: "Your dad says he doesn't know what happened; he was fine one second, and the next he was completely horizontal."

The others take over again, grimacing but seeming a bit too glad to be in a position of knowledge. They say that, before my father could catch himself, he slammed down hip-first, onto a rock. They say that when he tried to hoist himself, his leg wouldn't cooperate. He called out, but no one answered. They explain that he dragged himself all the way back up the hillside to his pickup, but when he got there, he couldn't get into the cab. Apparently he yelled; however, the other men were too far away to hear him, especially with the chain saw going.

"How long did he have to wait?" I ask, and they wince.

"It was probably at least two full hours," Mom says.

I shake my head now, imagining my seventy-eight-year-old father out there on the stiff half-frozen ground, staring up into the blue sky, just getting colder in his blue cotton work pants and jean jacket, hoping that one of the other woodcutters might emerge out of the forest. I imagine all this while my mother looks at me with a pained smile and while the doctors go on working down the hall, cutting Dad open from waist to knee, gathering the bone fragments into a bundle and wiring them around a long rod.

The circle of well-wishers are eager to be of help, so they offer a litany of meant-to-cheer-you-up quips: "Thank God someone went to get oil for the chainsaw." "Lord, yes. And it's a miracle he saw that pickup." "But I can't believe how strong your dad is—pulling himself up that hillside." "Amazing. Just like him, to be out there at that age, trying to help."

The surgery drags on, but five of the well-wishers

stay past midnight. They offer to go fetch coffee or to stand watch as I visit the basement snack shop. They are full of let-me-help eagerness. And since they are able to see any gesture I make or anything I might whisper to my mother, I don't have a chance to ask her how she is really doing.

I can tell that Mom is responding carefully, trying to keep up her best appearance, but I can also see that her energy is waning like the lights on a turned-off car, drained away by the very need to stay responsible. I am struggling myself, because I am dead-tired from a heavy week at work and from driving six hours. I am actually carrying my own secret burden, worn down by worries about being too absent lately with my sons—not present enough to know what is really going on inside of them. I would like to be getting Dad's advice right now, instead of sitting in a waiting room not sure whether he will recuperate.

As we wait deeper into the night, flanked by these other watchful well-wishers, part of me wants to shout, "I know that you care, but please go away!"

Three of them are people I don't even know. They are church goers whom I have not met in the years I have been away from Kansas, living in Iowa. If I have met them, it was only briefly, perhaps while buying groceries with my parents or taking them to the Chinese buffet over by the Holidome. And yet these three seem terribly pleased by their self-appointed helper role, as if thinking, *Look at me. I'm part of this little band of comrades, almost like a family. Isn't it great?*

Dad survives the surgery and is moved into ICU. He is terribly weakened and doesn't respond well to therapy or medication. His blood pressure won't stabilize. The doctors refuse to release him from Intensive Care even after five days. Technically, only family members should be allowed into his room. Yet visitors keep sneaking in, needing to connect, to fit in, to be part of the big clan of well-wishers.

The ones who come are not just long-standing friends, but an unpredictable assortment of odd acquaintances: an Ethiopian woman who wants to bring him her national food, a Viet Nam Vet who roofs houses and wants to show my father his pencil drawing of a white-tail deer, an extremely shy farmer who has carved a wooden crutch to help the recuperating patient. And though my weary mother sits outside in the hall trying to run interference, all too often she feels forced to go in and tell her husband that another visitor wants to say hello.

Dad, looking hollowed out and waxy, grimaces then swallows against the oxygen tubes. He hikes himself up, trying to appear prepared. When another person enters, he takes a terrible stab at smiling, lips chapped, face sagging, hand weakly lifted.

Of course, I admire his response. At some level I also appreciate what is happening with these guests—a kind of insistent homage. My father has always been an adopted father or brother for people outside the family, probably because he has shown such interest in whoever he met, especially those who would not normally get attention. I know that he has often stopped his afternoon walk to talk with a dour bachelor who collects water heaters in his yard. He has taken time to attend the high school graduation of a girl with cerebral palsy. Each Sunday, he has picked up and driven an Iranian graduate student to church. And now these "adopted" sons and daughters are flocking back to repay his kindnesses, not realizing that they are actually wearing him down.

The signs in the hall make it clear—"Only family allowed." However, no one seems to take the signs seriously. When Mom herself admits that the constant visits could do Dad in, I hand-letter another sign and tape it right in the middle of the Intensive Care door: "Our father is EXTREMELY tired. Please, no visitors!"

Finally, there is a respite, and the ailing man regains enough strength to be moved from Intensive Care. Finally, I can travel back to Iowa to see Cathleen and the boys and to teach classes for a few days. Yet I feel a weird mix of resentment and guilt when I return the next weekend and come down the hallway toward the new hospital room, as if I am returning to an abandoned post and must pay the consequences.

When I reach the doorway, sure enough, there is a young man in a chair on the far side of my father, and this man whom I have never met is laying a hand on Dad's shoulder saying a prayer. There is also an unfamiliar woman at the foot of the bed who has her head lowered, her hand resting on Dad's blanketed foot.

I wait there at the door until the couple has finished praying—"We just thank you, Lord, for the healing that you have brought, and we pray that you will continue to heal. We lift up our brother, knowing that he has been faithful and that you will be faithful. We thank you for the way he has touched our hearts. Please touch his own. Reach out and mend his body. In the name of Jesus, amen."

After the unfamiliar man has finished praying, he raises his head, opening his eyes. He has a dreamy faraway look. Then he sees me silhouetted in the door and lifts his brows, trying to figure out who this stranger might be. He rises from his chair, saying, "Well Charlie, I guess we'd better be going. Looks like you have another visitor."

Surprised, the man's wife and my bed-ridden father turn toward me. They appear puzzled. Dad even looks a bit dismayed.

For me, silhouetted in the doorway, it really does seem like I am just one more visitor in a long line. I have to admit that I have come wanting something too. Right now I feel like a screw-up, too often fixated on finding a better job, too often grouchy in the home, as if being a husband and a father were roles forced on me.

What's the trick, Dad? How were you so good at this stuff? That's what I want to ask. In that sense I am not unlike many of the others who have come. However, I don't want to be just another burden for him. With the young couple staring, I have an almost perverse urge to turn and walk away. I have to force myself to step forward out of the shadows, saying, "Hi Dad. I just got into town."

I feel a rush of gratefulness when he lights up, smiling in a way that suggests genuine pleasure. After I have introduced myself to the visiting couple and after I have asked how they know my father, I wait for them to say their goodbyes. Then I sit down, putting away my own problems, at least for now, and I ask the one question that most needs to be asked: "So, Dad, give me the straight scoop. How are you doing?"

Climbing Lesson 5

When we get the tent taken down and the backpacks organized, and when we drive the last hour to the trailhead, it is already past noon. Any half-wit could tell us we are idiots to start so late, but there is a kind of pleasure in ignoring conventional wisdom. We are flatlanders embracing our cluelessness. As hail starts thrashing us at timber line, we have to huddle under stunted trees, and we laugh. My brother Nat laughs and I laugh at him and at our youngest sons—lanky sixteen-year-olds who are thirty yards further up the slope trying to press themselves against a boulder, yelping as pebbles of ice ricochet off their heads and shoulders.

"Having fun?" we shout, and the teens begin to prance in place, long legs lifting in a jig.

There is great pleasure in seeing these two cousins—young men almost—bonded in mock misery. All the way out here, from the prairie to the mountains, there has been this deja-vu pleasure. Here is a mirroring that reminds me of when Nat and I were their age—the natural ease of two close friends, the love of a physical challenge, the glee of being pulled into horseplay.

This trip was not a mistake, I think, though I am worried about abandoning our still-recuperating father, who broke his hip months ago and is barely using a walker. I am also not sure I should be vacationing so close to starting the regimen of another school year. But no, this is not a mistake, I tell myself as the hail turns to freezing rain and I have to shuck off my pack, scrambling for a poncho.

The night before, when we had reached the mountains and driven halfway up the winding river canyon, Nat and I let our sons create a makeshift shelter down by the rapids, pulling a tarp over a taut cord then laying down river reeds as a mattress. We let them set up their own place next to the chuckling water, sharing whatever secrets they would want to share. And we enjoyed our own secrets, warming feet against the fire while doing something quite rare: smoking cigars. This was a bit of a tradition Nat had introduced on an earlier camping trip; just one cigar before going into the tent. So we rolled the smoke in our mouths and stared into the red, snapping coals and occasionally leaned back to savor the silhouetted ridges and the deep blue of the night, marveling at the array of incandescent stars.

The cigars, and the galaxy above, turned us philosophical.

"So what's next in life?" Nat asked from his log, leaning back from the smoke, his stocky legs stretched toward the flames. "What do you have on your list?"

If another man had asked, I might have taken this question as a competitive challenge—as if there was a need to prove myself—but I knew better. I was conscious that Nat was asking this question after being laid off at an organization where he had worked for twenty years, facilitating social services for people with blindness. For twenty years he had cheerfully and faithfully helped blind youth get placed at specialized schools. He had written grants that subsidized eye surgeries and equipment that would assist the blind. Basically, he had been the sort of relational, caring person we all wish we could be—only to get the rug pulled out from under him. Fifty-years-old and forced to start over on a new career, managing a research project through an extension program at Kansas State University, a project focused on drought-resistant sorghum rather than services for the blind.

"I don't know. Why do you ask?"

"I guess it's because right now I don't even know how to think in goals," Nat replied, his eyes glittering in the shadows under his prominent brow. "It's like nothing's in the tank."

I sat quiet for a while, poking at a log with my toe

and sending a column of sparks into the darkness. I was thinking about how obsessed I had become with securing a better teaching position—sending off resumes and letters of reference and sample syllabi. Lately I had felt like I was inside a huge gerbil wheel of my own making, basically sacrificing today on the altar of tomorrow. This trip had shown me how little time I had actually spent with Luke the past year—not just the expected school events but true together-time.

"Maybe goals are overrated," I murmured. "Maybe it's like they all say: relationships matter. I mean you've always seemed to get that right, taking time to do stuff with your kids. Camping like this. Letting your kids bring friends over."

"Yeah, but it would be nice to have a plan, too. More of a next step, and next."

When they have pulled ponchos down over their shoulders, covering their packs as well, our sons leave the shelter of the boulder. Like fantastic long-legged humpbacks, they continue up the mountain in the downpour, sloshing along a trail that has turned into a small stream. We follow a bit more slowly, feeling the burn of the high altitude, the sagging weight of the packs and the stiffening in our knees. It's good to be able to keep up with these boys somewhat, but we are tired enough to climb cautiously, concentrating on the rocky slope, taking quick glances to see how much closer we are getting to the big bowl that is supposed to be up above us, where all the snowmelt of three peaks gathers into a set of small lakes.

"I found some cigarettes in one of the boy's packs," Nat suddenly says. "I think they're my guy's."

What to say? It's a bit of a shock. Luke hasn't seemed to be inclined that way, but what if he was the one to bring the cigarettes. And then there's the whole double standard of the cigars last night, which I enjoyed but kind of hoped my son wasn't seeing.

"I suppose either one of them could have brought them." I say.

"Except Alex has been doing stuff like this more and more. Hiding things. He's always got something up his sleeve. That's the part that ticks me off. So I told them that, if they brought stuff along, they ought to at least share."

I laugh. This is as good an answer as any. I like my brother and the ease with which he talks to the two guys. I admire the cheerful rapport he keeps despite the tough situation he's been through. I like my nephew Alex too—a curious kid with a quiet interest in nature, legendary for his ability to stalk wild birds or name trees. A mischievous kid who often smiles like he's got something hidden in his mouth.

Yesterday, as we were driving up to the campsite in the canyon, we decided to pull off the main road and stop at a nearby lake for a bit of late-afternoon fishing. The only thing any of us caught were crawdads, which clenched on the bait and wouldn't let go until they had been reeled in. Then, while I was changing to a spinner, hoping that something flashy might capture attention, I saw Alex around a bend, standing out in the lake up to his knees. Ever so slowly the teen leaned over and reached into the water, slipping his hands and forearms down into the snowmelt cold. And then he stayed there, bent over for six or seven minutes—long enough to make me stop fishing and simply marvel.

That water was bone-shrinking cold, yet my nephew seemed completely unaffected, still as a rock. Until... as sudden as a tripped snare, he yanked upward and flung a live trout ten feet onto the shore, dashing after it in his sandals and shorts so that he could snatch it before it flopped back into the lake.

I whistled just to get Alex's attention, then lifted both thumbs. And he gave me one of his patented I-swallowed-a-canary grins. It was beautiful what he had done, but also sad in a strange way, as if he had disappeared out of all human connection for a while due to his steely resolve.

When Alex acted as if he might toss the fish back into the lake, I called out, "Hey, hey, that's a keeper. We can cook it for supper." I wanted him to keep the trout so that Luke and Nat could hear the story. I wanted him to lift the fish out in front of him and jog back around the corner, ready to answer all the inevitable questions. Instead, he shrugged and slid a stringer through the trout's gills. Then he stood there as if he had forgotten what he intended to do, and I felt a stab of guilt for having disrupted his natural state.

Finally the hail and rain let up, and Nat and I come over a last rise to find a jumpable stream and our sons laying out the tent with a silver mirror of a lake at their backs. The boys are triumphant, having outpaced us by a good ten minutes. I get smack-talk from Luke, who is enjoying having his cousin to boast with: "What's with all the heavy-breathing, Mr. Mountain Man?" He thumps me on the back, one corner of his mouth lifted sardonically. "You sure you don't need some CPR?"

What Luke doesn't anticipate is that Nat and I will work in telepathic unison, gripping him and lifting him into the air and carrying him by his armpits and beltloops toward the lake, to demonstrate that, in fact, we still have more energy than might be expected. He shouts with alarm as we swing him back and forth toward the water, counting "One," "Two," "Three..." And it's clear he loves the goofy adrenaline rush of the moment.

We are all laughing, and it is perfect... that is, until

the rain pours down again and the not-yet-erected tent is lying out gathering puddles, forcing us to fumble with frigid fingers, sliding poles into position then battening on the fly so that we can toss our muddy packs inside and climb in shivering.

So there we are for the rest of the evening, huddled around a propane cooking flame and peeling off wet clothes. We slide into semi-wet sleeping bags to gripe good-naturedly about the insanity of the situation we have gotten ourselves into. And when we try to sleep at last, the tent that was roomy just a night earlier—with two inside—is far too small for four grown males. Even after we have shoved the packs outside into the rain, swaddled in ponchos, three of us must lie sideways, spooning together, and the fourth—the quiet, fish-snatching, cigarette-smuggling nephew who has volunteered for the worst position—must sleep across the back of the tent, knees bent in the air, body bumping the tops of our heads as he shifts.

It is hard to sleep, and there is a lot of adjusting and grumbling. Then someone farts and we all groan. After a while, though, I hear my son starting to snore, sinuses stuffed up by allergies, and when no one comments, I realize they are succumbing to sleep as well.

I feel my nephew's knees sag onto my head. I try to ignore the weight and the sawing and snorts. I try to release myself into badly-needed rest. For a moment I drift into a bizarre dream about holding a frog in my cupped palms and walking to a cliff edge with surf below, breaking on the rocks. The frog suddenly leaps out of my hands, falling, falling, falling down onto the rocks, where I am absolutely sure, suddenly, that it is *not* a frog but my own son.

Terrified, I jerk to the surface of consciousness, hearing my heart pound. I stare into the utter blackness of the tent, still gripped by the dread of having let my child leap out of my hands. Then I hear Luke snort beside me and I hear the others breathing more regularly. The adrenaline wears off, so I sink back toward relaxation.

I am slipping toward unconsciousness again—and just about to go under—when I once more sit up gasping. This time, though, I realize what is happening: My lungs won't let me fall asleep because they are struggling for oxygen. The altitude is taking revenge.

For a while, I just lie there in the blackness feeling myself pull at thin air and sensing that this most elemental, unconscious habit is failing me. I am overcome by a wave of vertigo then nausea.

This trip has not been a mistake. I know that. Today, despite the hail and the rain and even this miserable moment, I am convinced that this is the best thing I have done in a long while. I should be doing more of it actually. It's terrific to have seen my son, no longer aloof, drop his head and charge into me after being nearly tossed in the lake. To have seen him roll in his sleeping bag right over the top of his cousin, then get flung off and steam-rolled in return. Or to have watched the two boys taking turns stealing macaroni and tuna out of each other's bowls, stabbing and deflecting each other's cutlery.

So why the concurrent sense of dread?

Both of these boys are getting older, I think. They are no longer the cute youngest children who willingly joined whatever the parents or the older siblings wanted to do. They are no longer the lap-boys who loved a head-scratch, listening quietly to the mill of adult conversation. They have their own agendas, their desire to be something "other." I have seen it in Luke already—how he is inclined to call me after school, asking if he can go home with a friend, often someone I have never met.

I know it's happening with my nephew too—maybe in even more pronounced ways, given how scarce Nat says the boy has become. Apparently, Alex has been disappearing for whole afternoons and evenings with a cluster of guys who share a love of out-of-bounds places like an abandoned ruin on the edge of town or a fishing hole they found just inside the grounds of the military reservation, where a swing-down gate says "No Trespassing: Army Training Grounds."

These friends are easy-going guys with long shocks of hair and lanky limbs. My brother says they interact in a good way but seem too laid-back, as if nothing matters enough to make them alert. And though Nat hasn't wondered it out loud, he is probably questioning, just like I am questioning as I sit in this claustrophobic darkness: Are those friends of my nephew, when they get together, smoking something stronger than cigarettes?

Exhausted, I am swept by another wave of nausea. This time I have to lean forward and unzip the tent fly, poking my head out in case of vomit. To my surprise, the air outside the tent, though cold, feels richer with oxygen. I have a stocking hat on, so I leave my head out there, carefully realigning myself and placing my feet where my head used to be. I put an arm out to rest my head upon. I stare at the bright moonlight on the rocks and the trees—so bright that I can almost see the greenness in the leaves of a nearby sapling—and when I open my eyes again, it is 8:00 in the morning and the sun is over the mountain ridge and a chipmunk is bobbing on a log only three feet away, pulsing its tail as if getting ready to make a leap.

I turn my head to find my brother tending a smoky fire with wet twigs and bits of paper and a carton from last night's dinner packages. The two boys are harder to spot, far off on the opposite shore of the lake in their bright yellow and red stocking hats. They seem to be swinging something overhead then throwing it across the water. Behind them, a pair of ragged mountain peaks rip into the blue sky, huge rocky crags that have shucked off all the splintered rocks below and the little heaps of white snow. The peaks, lit up by the rising sun, are wonderfully crisp in the thin air.

"Hey bro, I thought you lost your head when I woke up and saw just your shoulders down there by my feet."

"Man, there was no oxygen in that tent. You guys used it all up."

"Well, it apparently didn't affect the boys. They're off fishing already. I guess they thought to bring some string and hooks, and they made bobbers out of sticks. They're using a hot dog for bait."

Across the water comes a sudden whoop, and we both look up to see our sons celebrating together—leaning over and talking excitedly then straightening for a high-five. I hope that maybe, this time, it is Luke who has caught the fish. I know how happy that would make him.

"Like two peas in a pod," says my brother Nat. "You know, we are not going to get a lot more chances like this. Another year or two and they are going to be launched. Last ones out of the nest."

"Yeah, it's terrific seeing them together. They've always had something special. Same quietness. Same sense of humor. I'm glad we made it out here—for them."

"For us, too," says Nat, pulling back from the little tepee of twigs and paper, which has blossomed into flame. "This, bro, is the life!"

Nothing about that morning on the lakeside, with the kindling crackling to life and the boys shouting across the lake and the sunshine warming my chilled face, nothing about it suggested the phone call that would come a year later from Nat.

"I've got some bad news," I would hear in the phone receiver, gathering not just the content but the tone—so tender and eerily sad that surely it was about our ailing father, who had barely survived his broken hip a year and a half earlier.

I would steel myself, readying for the expected news. But nothing about that glorious morning in the mountains could prepare me for what would come: "I can't believe I'm even saying this, but Alex died today."

There would be no trail to follow after that. No trail—in the days and weeks and years to come—that would lead through the waiting wilderness. No way to track down the boy who had swallowed all his secrets and disappeared.

Notes from the Bleachers

We have brought Luke on his first college visit—at a well-established Lutheran college in northern Iowa—and we are in the auditorium as he is recognized for a potential scholarship. All the visiting students have been offered scholarships, and they are being welcomed in an innovative way—through quick blurbs they wrote for themselves. Most of the blurbs mention accomplishments like studying in Sweden as an exchange student, accumulating a 3.9 GPA, or placing at the state track meet in high jump. Some are humorous, though. And our son's brings a riot of laughter.

Luke is walking across the stage as the blurb is read, and the main thing that is noticeable about him, aside from his lanky thinness, is his amazing head of hair. It is a sculpted ball of curly brown hair that stands up another two or three inches off his head, afro-style. Combined with his tall thinness, it makes him look a bit like a human lollipop, which is central to the laughter, since his particular blurb goes as follows: "Our next scholarship recipient, Luke Bascom, has one claim to fame. On a class visit to the Iowa state capitol, he was given a golden hair pick from the Governor, who officially dubbed him 'the student with most impressive hair in the entire state'."

Cathleen and I give each other a grin, enjoying the comedic side of our son. We are pleased that he is a maverick, not afraid to poke fun at himself or at the college's invitation to show off. We are proud of his alternative-rock attitude. But we are also, like any parents, forced to see him as he appears today, against the backdrop of all these other prospective college students.

I note, from up there in the auditorium seats, that Luke walks with shoulders slightly hunched. I note that, though the audience is laughing, Luke is hardly smiling. I note that, unlike other young men and women who have come onto the stage with confident swagger, my son is fixed on getting his scholarship certificate and simply getting off the stage.

Luke has always been shy, so a bit of awkwardness is to be expected. However, he has always been a cheerful, handsome fellow with his own quiet energy. He's not the kid that I am seeing out there on the stage, where all the focused attention has forced me to watch with new eyes.

This sardonic humor and bushy hair go with a persona that has only recently emerged—after the death of Luke's closest cousin and after the loss of his girlfriend, who was a year older, gorgeous, and not at all hesitant to dump him as soon as she graduated high school and set her sights on becoming a sorority girl. Now, instead of hanging out at her million-dollar house with her attorney parents or with her slightly-older friends, Luke has become devoted to new bandmates in a group called "Quick Piss"—a laid-back but edgy group of long hairs who play driven songs that verge on punk. He has dropped soccer too, even though he played it all the way through junior high and high school.

For the past year, Luke has been gone a lot in the evenings, practicing with Quick Piss at the house of the lead singer, who has an apt first name: "Stone." Luke has kept playing with his brother's band too, but mainly he has been performing with this new group, going out to the few bars in Des Moines that allow minors to play before nine o'clock. When he performs now, he thrashes the drums with an angry intensity that suggests he is trying to beat them into submission.

Here's the thing. I see Luke down there on the college stage with all the other potential students and their Swedish Lutheran blondeness, and I can tell he doesn't really want to shine, at least not in the airbrushed way that they do—the guys with styled hair and neat slacks, the girls with high heels and tight dresses. My son is down there in worn corduroys and a flannel shirt, looking like someone forced him to come to this event, which is probably the case.

Face it, I realize, he is probably down there because we expected it of him. And by now, it's clear he will NOT be choosing this college, with its monochrome Lutheran population and its excellent this and excellent that. I don't even have to ask him to know that he has checked this institution off his list. And that's okay really. I understand his desire to not be safe, predictable, conformist. I even applaud. I have always wanted Luke and Conrad to be freethinkers, not swayed by the status quo. I have wanted them to see through the American illusions of materialism and success at all costs. However, I also don't want that swim-against-the-current attitude to block their potential or their possibilities in life.

So it's hard sitting up there in the bleachers and watching. I know how smart this guy is and how musically gifted and hard-working. I know how prematurely wise he is—always watching others closely and arriving at carefully-thought-out conclusions. I know how loyal he can be, and how much of a diplomat he is, trying to bring peace to the people around him. I know he is quiet but quick with wit. I know he is incredibly fast on the soccer field, able to outstrip chasing defenders and nail the ball into the corner of the net. I know he is sensitive and affectionate underneath the calluses that have begun to form, and I don't want that sensitive affection to get forced back into a closet, even though I understand the losses that might cause such a retreat.

I clap along with all the other parents, as each young person takes the stage, but my attention is still on that one young man sitting now with the others in the front row of the auditorium, his big brown poof of hair setting him apart. That guy, that's the one I want to shine in his own unique, wonderfully gifted way. That's the one who I am really applauding.

A Grand Sort of Magic

Our older son Conrad, now twenty-two, is taking an indefinite break from college, having decided to give his full attention to music. He doesn't want to look back and regret never really trying.

For a bit he is renting a room in Des Moines and working as a janitor at a funky craft shop that makes high-end decorative furniture. At night, he tends bar at his favorite music venue, trying to pull together money for recording songs. He doesn't answer his cell phone, although sometimes he calls a day later to apologize. And if he comes over for dinner, he tends to stay only until a text message pulls him away.

How is he really doing? I'm not sure, since he has become so resolutely independent. As a result, it is interesting to see the transformation that occurs when we travel as a family back to Kansas at Thanksgiving. When we step onto the porch of my parents' log house, this long-haired, cool musician lets go of his usual non-expressive exterior. He suddenly becomes playful, growling and harrumphing as he shifts into a weightlifter's stance. His grandfather—now over eighty—puts aside the aluminum walker and spreads his arms. Then he grunts as he pulls Conrad into a giant bear hug, actually lifting him off his feet.

Not to be outdone, our son tries to return the favor. His grandpa is now a gaunt and brittle version of the top-heavy man he once was. His trousers are baggy round his shrinking girth, and he is stooped. But Conrad makes a big deal of the tremendous effort it takes to get this old man into the air. Then he gives up with a groan, and there is laughter all round. Both men beat their chests King-Kong style, and Luke steps in to join the ritual, bumping his chest against theirs.

I know that Dad would not approve of bartending. If he went to the place where Conrad serves drinks, he would look askance at the raunchy band posters and the dark dancing. And if he could hear Conrad perform, he would be distressed by the frank language. But it is obvious that he loves this young man deeply—and feels a special bond to him.

In fact, the two are so linked that sometimes they disappear together. On Thanksgiving morning, after I have struggled to sleep, I get up and see that, surprisingly, Conrad is not in the other guestroom, across from his snoring brother. I don't find Conrad until I have heated a kettle and made some tea and glanced out the kitchen window onto the front porch. There he sits with his grandfather, the two of them still in PJ bottoms gesticulating.

Only after the rest of the family has come downstairs and eaten half their breakfast, do these two finish their "one-on-one." And then they come into the house grinning, saying, "You first." "No, you first." "No, I insist." "But I insist even more," –until they must take the aluminum walker and inch it forward together, squeezing through the doorway simultaneously.

I smile in response to these hijinks, happy to see Conrad up early and talking animatedly. I ask if the two of them have solved the world's problems, and I get a sarcastic reply: "Only global hunger. We still need another hour to take care of the Mid-East."

The fact is that they have actually been out on the porch with a Bible, reading verses and discussing them. I know this because I have done it so many times myself while growing up. And that makes the morning meeting more surprising—since I also know that Conrad is basically an agnostic. If I were to suggest we have an hour of Bible reading and discussion before breakfast, it would *never* happen, but with Grandpa Charles, some sort of elder magic has prevailed.

Conrad's obvious delight makes me recall how, in church years ago, when he was still a smooth-faced junior high boy, I passed by his Sunday School classroom just as he replied to a teacher's question: "Who is your spiritual hero?"

His response was quick, "My grandfather. The one on my dad's side."

"And why?"

"Because he practices what he preaches. He cares about everybody and shows it all the time."

Indeed, I think, as I watch Conrad sit down at the table, comically placing all the food items in a circle around his grandfather's plate: the bowl of oatmeal, the raisins, the honey, the pitcher of milk, the biscuits, the jam. Luke joins in, adding butter, bananas, orange juice. And the two of them get thanked solemnly by Dad, who is a hollowed-out version of himself but still knows how to play along: "Quite kind of you. Yes. Yes. And could you add some corn flakes? Don't forget the bacon, either."

There is still much to be learned from this patriarch, not only for his near-adult grandsons but me, the middle-aged man who is trying to figure out how to play the fathering role. I watch as Conrad and Luke take turns buttering their grandfather's biscuit and pouring orange juice for him and adding milk to his coffee. I laugh along with my mother and my wife. Part of me is almost jealous, but another part is very, very glad.

What Goes Around...

All I have done is to tousle Luke's bountiful hair, grabbing a handful and tugging just as I have done a thousand times when playfully saying goodnight or when trying to help him stay alert while prepping for exams. So it is hard to have him jerk back, brushing my hand away.

To see his involuntary grimace? Even harder.

What I want to do is to get back in the car and head home, despite the fact that Cathleen and I have driven across three states expressly to see his dorm and to ask how classes are going, talking about whatever might be divulged. These days it seems everything is on a need-to-know basis. It seems contact is limited to texting, even though this is the hang-out boy who used to love spending whole Saturday afternoons on the couch, watching college football games with me.

How can this be the same guy, I wonder, and when did this near revulsion emerge?

Then, with a shudder, I recall a long-ago gathering in a restaurant parking lot, when I was about to get in a car with a high-school friend and leave for my first semester of college. I remember how my father called us into a huddle—the parents of the other guy, my mother, both sets of siblings—and how Dad instructed the group to surround me and the other college-bound guy, squeezing us into a giant hug, not just once but three times. I remember the curious amusement of a passing girl. And the way a middle-aged man pointed with his chin, getting his wife to chuckle.

The mother of my friend had her face squashed against my chest. My dad's face was close enough for me to smell the maple syrup he had eaten on his pancakes. It was all supposed to be fun and funny, but how I despised the forced intimacy. Dad's close, sweet breath made me desperate to explode out of the circle.

And now, looking over at my own please-don't-touch-me son, I realize there must be thousands, no hundreds of thousands of teen sons sitting beside fathers in the same recoiling way, many of them in dorms all over the nation. Sons who have reached the moment when they have to pull away whether they want to or not. Sons realizing that it is time to make their own run at this thing called "being a man." Sons with testosterone rising inside them like sap. Sons who want to say, "Dad, don't touch me like you are still in charge."

I can't help it—I want to get in the car and drive away. I am thinking, *Go ahead; stand on your own feet! See how far you get.*

However, I stay seated on the lower bunk of the dorm room with the boy to my side—no, the young man. I glance over and realize he is now an inch taller than me, sturdy-jawed, with a handsome crest of brown hair. I look over and think about the fact that he is now making all his own pocket money, working at the music library on campus and asking girls out when he feels like it—girls I have never met. I glance up at my wife, who is smiling at me in a be-patient sort of way, and I finally ask, "So, guy, what's the best part of being in college?"

Such a Quiet, Quiet House

"Are the cats a compensation?" asks my therapist.

"A what?"

"Are they a replacement for your sons?"

I snort. Ridiculous. I am not one of those pets-as-children people. Cats don't talk, play drums, bring girls home for prom pictures, run off to college, leave you feeling abandoned.

And yet... when I come home from work a few days later and Cathleen is not back from her job, it is true that I find myself on the couch in the den talking to the two cats, asking them how their day went and whether they did anything interesting or just laid around watching the sunlight creep across the carpet.

I talk especially to the kitten, who keeps turning on my lap and climbing my belly to look into my eyes as if wondering what's back there. This kitten, which we supposedly got as a companion for the older cat, is in motion constantly, biting at the pen I use to grade papers or climbing my torso onto my shoulders so that he can chew on an earlobe. And when I look up from the couch at the portrait of our sons painted by a close friend, I realize that, yes, maybe these two cats *are* a sort of compensation. I would never admit it, of course, but yes, maybe I agreed to add a kitten because I was secretly wanting something that might be provided, at least a little bit, by a little tumbling, motor-in-the-mouth ball of fur.

The kitten seems to have severe attention deficit disorder plus hyperactivity. It is constantly leaping toward whatever causes a distraction: a moving shoe, a dropped pad of paper, a reflection on the TV screen. It attacks my shirt, pulling the buttons. It bites the glasses off my face. It leaps right through the newspaper when I open it.

The older cat, by contrast, likes to snuggle, leaving the couch when things get too rowdy. She jumps down and walks to the easy chair, looking back as if to say, "Aren't you coming?" She springs up there and rolls onto her back, exposing her belly, which she knows I cannot resist. So I cross over the den and sit down with this calmer, older creature, who stretches luxuriously as I scratch her soft underside. After a minute, she rolls onto her stomach again and stays right there against my thigh, purring as I finger her ears and scratch her chin. Contact and affection, she loves this treatment, not unlike Luke, who used to come over and flop onto one of our laps, lifting the tail of his shirt for a back scratch.

The kitten, on the other hand, he's more like our older son, who was always more restless, in need of stimulation. I remember taking Conrad to church as a one-year-old, and how I used to have to turn him in my arms as if running a rotisserie. I would hold him belly-up, then belly-down, then hoist him onto a shoulder, looking back at parishioners. And now, here is this kitten, who has a kind of obsessive-compulsive need to climb up, roll over, flop down, turn, butt with his head, grab at every object with his paws, and gnaw, gnaw, gnaw. And I am amused, pleasantly distracted by all his action.

I look across the room to the portrait of our two sons, arms over each others' shoulders, smiling, and I can almost hear an echo: "Daddy, I wanna backscratch. I wanna head scratch. I wanna play. Let's be knights and fight swords. Let's make a boat. Let's make a bear trap. Let's make clay films like *Wallace and Gromit*. Let's lay down and stare at the clouds...."

Every day was so "alive" with the two of them. Every day was exhausting but also varied, rich with imaginative demands. And now? Here I sit on a couch in an empty house, time on my hands.

"Hey, I'm home," calls my wife from the back door. "You here?" And for a moment I don't answer.

It's not nice of me, I know. But she is not the boys.

She is the domestic partner who keeps padding the nest and making me aware it is empty. She is the sweet, gentle "other" who doesn't want anyone throwing a football near the china hutch.

She'll want us to decide whether spaghetti or stir fry, whether dishes or laundry, red wine or white. If we make love tonight, which I vaguely hope, it will be making love for the thousandth time. Yes, I want this to happen. I still find pleasure in our romantic play. But there is something redundant about everything now, and something that she simply can't supply, something I find myself missing.

The kitten jumps up onto my lap again and ventures onto a knee, perching where the leg is bent and crossed over. The tiny creature tight-ropes on my elevated shin until he reaches my tennis shoe, where he tugs at the shoelaces, starting to pull them untied, doing something aggressive and charming in an I'm-going-to-mess-with-you way.

"Should we tell her where we are?" I whisper.

No reply from the kitten, but I wait a few more seconds, watching the creature tear at my shoelaces... until at last I shout, "Hey, we're in here, babe! Me and you-guess-who."

Drafts in the Desk Drawer

~~Dear boys sons young men~~ Guys,

I'm not sure what I'm trying to say here, but that is probably no surprise. ~~Maybe~~ I've never been sure about much really, even when I have wanted to seem ~~perfectly~~ confident about something—whether it was insisting you could not order soft drinks ~~(water is healthier and cheaper, by the way)~~ or demanding that you go to bed by a certain hour. I was always inclined to buckle. That's because ~~I could see the other side and because~~ I have always been instinctually against dogmatism, even in myself....

Guys,

Okay, let me ~~try again~~ start over. Sometimes I wish I had been a better model when it comes to faith.

I know, you're smirking. And I know that you

probably think this is about me and my need to get resolution on my childhood. And maybe you're partly right. Yes, I found it hard to have parents who seemed so sure of their beliefs—as if my own spiritual identity had been pre-scripted and foreclosed. And yes, I know that you ~~understand because you~~ have had your own moments of feeling ~~trapped~~ coerced when we took you to church weekly or when we visited the grandparents, who expected you to automatically volunteer for prayers at dinner, to lament the decline of America, or to eagerly talk about Bible passages.

~~Yes, I have been conflicted about how I was raised, but on the other hand,~~ Here's the thing, though. You may not understand this since you are not my age and have not become parents yet, but I can see now that my parents gave me a kind of stability just by being who they were—rock-steady, faithful people. So I guess I'm saying that (as a parent who did a kind of pendulum swing to the other side) I may not have done you a favor. I'm saying that, even though I'm a doubter, I don't wish doubting on you. ~~I'm saying that sometimes I see your own questioning, challenging, agnostic tendencies and just feel bad because, really, we all need something to believe in.~~

Hi again,

This may be a surprise ~~to you~~, but the fact is that,

even though I have always struggled spiritually, I have also had a buried, bedrock sort of belief in the creator behind this marvel of a world. The stars in space, the bluegills in the lake, the way maples do their multitudinous leafy thing in the spring, the way I am talking to you right now and you are, for the most part, understanding—that doesn't seem accidental to me.

No, I don't feel like I can define who is behind it all, and I am suspicious of people who act cock-sure about such definitions, as if they could draw you a picture. I'm skeptical. However, at the same time I have always hoped you would have at least this much assurance in your life, if not more. I have hoped you would be able to affirm your own beliefs better than me—ideally because they weren't foisted off on you.

Here's the thing. ~~though. Although I may seem "tortured" in this area, you don't have to be. I'm okay if you just want to affirm what you believe.~~ I'd actually be happy if you each found your own spiritual path—because it's hard to live without faith. It's better, it seems to me, to be able to believe and to operate out of belief. We all need some framework that guides our decisions and actions, some perspective that gives us hope when we rise in the morning. That's what I most want for you.

Love,

Dad

P.S.—~~I guess~~ It's not easy to say exactly what I mean because it's like trying to talk about another language—a really beautiful language—while not being able to speak it very well. I want you to have that language even if I don't. I think, when it all boils down, that's the essence of what I'm trying to say.

Intensive Care

For three days and nights our whole clan has been occupying a visiting room in the Intensive Care Unit at Mercy Hospital in Manhattan, Kansas, sometimes falling asleep on the carpeted floor while waiting to see if our patriarch will survive. I am there with my wife and two grown sons. Both my brothers are there with their wives and kids. Together, we are twelve—or thirteen if you throw in our mom, the matriarch, who is generally sitting in the patient room right next to her semi-comatose husband.

The doctors are keeping the eighty-four-year-old sedated since they have him intubated and have installed a heart pump that is doing half the work of the damaged organ. On those occasions when meds wear off, he emerges groggily, strapped down, jerking in his restraints, eyes roving.

He can't speak due to the oxygen tube in his mouth and throat. He tries to talk around it, and we keep telling him, "Be patient, Dad. We know you want to say something but you have to wait a bit longer, until things are more stable. Soon, hopefully."

He shuts his eyes in frustration then opens them and looks around wildly. He tries to lift his hand, which is strapped to the bar on the side of the bed so that he won't pull out the ventilator tube. Then he pinches two fingers together with his thumb and wiggles the fingers in a gesture that suggests handwriting, so we grab a clipboard and put a pen in his fingers. Since he can't lift his head and can't lift an arm to write, he must work by feel. The pen forms what might be a J then a T (or another J), followed by an N. It doesn't make sense to us, so he keeps scribbling. This time it might be a couple words. However, since he can't move his strapped wrist, everything piles up, becoming a snarled scribble.

Stepping in, my brother Nat tries to move the clipboard as Dad writes, hoping the words will separate into a proper sentence. However, the result is as readable as an electrocardiogram.

"Sorry Dad, we can't quite tell what you're writing."

A frustrated lowering of the brows. A tapping of the pen on the clipboard as if to say, "C'mon, pay attention." Then those individual letters again, in loose cursive: J, T, and N.

My older brother, John, finally gets it and asks: "Are you using our initials to tell us who we are? Is that what you're doing?"

We see a slight nod, and we congratulate him. "Good job. That's great to know—that you are still thinking straight and know who's here. We're glad. We hope we can take that tube out of your throat soon and talk."

Another weary nod. Then a closing of the eyes. Though the pen is still on the paper, it slips, leaving a wavy line.

It's been three days and nights since the massive heart attack. He was apparently asleep in bed then rolled over groaning, "Heart attack. The real thing. Gotta go."

Nat, who had moved into a house next to our parents, took the call from Mom and ran over to carry Dad into the car at two in the morning, not waiting for an ambulance. He drove the ten miles to Mercy Hospital at 90 miles an hour and said he could hear Dad in back trying the whole way to sing a hymn:

"To God be the glory, great things He has done;

So loved He the world that He gave us His Son..."

Nat said our father would break off in pain then pick up again, half-sighing, just whispering the tune into the dark cab of the car, using it like a woman might use breathing in Lamaze:

"Praise the Lord, praise the Lord,

Let the earth hear His voice!"

Apparently, he was still singing when they put him onto the gurney and rolled him into the hospital, the same hospital where his own father, Doc K.F., had done surgery forty years earlier:

"Praise the Lord, praise the Lord,

Let the people rejoice!"

An Emergency Room Technician came running, telling him to relax, they had him now and they would do everything to get him through this. This EMT was a big line-backer-of-a-man with weightlifter arms, and when Dad saw him, he reached up just enough to give him a half-hug, as if he was reuniting with an old family member. Then he clenched his face, closed his eyes, and went Code Blue.

"It was classic," said Nat. "Trying to connect even while he was on the verge of dying."

We all chuckle, staring down at our aged father in his hospital bed—mouth open around the ventilator tube, eyes occasionally moving under their lids, arms twitching. Everyone is worn out by the strain of waiting so long and wondering, and by the sheer pain of seeing our family leader strapped down with that tube in his throat. We are glad he is trying to communicate, but we are emotionally exhausted by the attempt to decode what he is saying, also by the attempt to stay upbeat, ignoring the wretchedness of what he must be feeling. This is the third heart scare, going all the way back to the time of his broken hip, when the doctors found a blocked artery and had to put in a stent. He's had three stent procedures since then, coming out weaker each time but never so severely incapacitated. For Dad, being able to talk—to connect with others—is everything, and now even that has been denied.

When the assigned hospitalist comes into the room, my brothers and my mom and I gather around her, asking questions. Any progress on his heart function? Can the ventilator tube come out? What about the pump?

She is sober. She explains that, though they had been hoping for the heart to return to a more robust pumping, it hasn't, and it probably won't. She says she understands the desire to let him talk, but the pump and the ventilator are actually what may be keeping him alive. She says that, in fact, it's unfortunate but the heart pump needs to come out soon. Using it too long could lead to a rupture or could make the artery turn septic.

Being the most blunt member of the family, I ask, "Are you telling us that we might lose him when it comes out?"

She nods.

"And are you saying that we should still go ahead and remove it?"

She nods again. "Very soon. We recommend it comes out within 48 hours, and we're way past that."

My brother John clears his throat, his silver hair in a tumble and his eyes heavy with pouches of fatigue: "The pump, yes. But can the ventilator tube stay in? Will that help?"

The hospitalist replies, "It could lengthen things, give him a better shot. But it will mean he still can't talk."

Everyone is quiet now, thinking, letting the news settle in.

"I don't know what you guys think, and Mom, you haven't said anything," I say, "but I think Dad wouldn't want to be stuck unable to talk to us. If this is it, I think he would want that tube out of his mouth."

We are all quiet again, thinking. I am thinking too, realizing there is a good chance my father won't be alive in a few hours. I am thinking, I knew this was going to happen but not today. I'm not ready. Dad is the buffer zone. He stands in between me and my own mortality. He lets me still be a son.

"Mom?" says Nat, settling one of his sturdy hands on her shoulder. "What do you think? What would Dad want?"

She looks at the three of us with eyes that are welling. She takes a broken breath and grits her teeth. She says, "He would want to talk."

"Okay, then," says the hospitalist, crossing arms over her blue scrubs. "If I'm hearing correctly, you are in agreement with the decision to remove the heart pump, and you would like the ventilator tube removed too. You understand that there's a fifty-fifty chance here, since we just don't know how his body will react. There is a chance he'll bounce back and start to make it on his own. There is also the chance we'll lose him. But you would like to be able to talk with him, and you feel that he would want that. Am I right?"

Mom nods, and so do we, as we stand around her, up against the railing of the hospital bed. Then, when I look down at my father—jowls sagging, skin clammy and pale—I begin to cry. Helping to decide his fate was not part of the deal when I left home three nights ago. But here I am, looking at my own father and suggesting that, even if it kills the man, we ought to let him have one last chance to be in control—to think clearly and say what he wants.

It's the right decision. I know that. I just don't want to live with the results.

An hour later, the tubes are out and the sedation is wearing off. We can see our mother in the room leaning over Dad, giving him a kiss on the forehead.

She gestures us into the room, so we go in, followed by the heart surgeon who took out the heart pump. We stand in a row by his bed and Mom says, "Honey, here are your sons and the cardiologist who has been taking care of your heart."

He shifts his head slowly to look all the way down the line of men, ending with the surgeon—a short thin man from India.

He wrinkles his brow then asks in a scratchy

whisper, "Which one is the doctor?"

John and Nat and I glance at each other with anguished grimaces. So it's happening. He's losing his mental faculties.

However, our father smiles wryly and whispers, "I know which one!"

We laugh. We cry. We wag our fingers at him, which makes him smile a little more.

He is having a hard time breathing or swallowing but he wants to know certain things. He asks the surgeon, "Was it a widow-maker?"

The surprised doctor, not knowing this phrase, looks to the hospitalist, who just came into the room. She laughs. "That's not a term we use any longer, Dr. Bascom. For obvious reasons. But yes, it would qualify as a widow maker."

Then he asks where the EMT is—the one who used the paddles on him.

"You can actually remember him?" Nat asks. "I thought you were out."

Dad opens his mouth in a painful "O" and scrunches his brows. "If they used the paddles on you, I bet you'd remember." He swallows painfully, takes another breath. "I just kept thinking, if it's gonna hurt this much, mind if I scream?"

We laugh again, and he grins, glad to be himself. He actually seems deliriously happy lying there on the bed with the tube out of his mouth, alive, able to say things to his wife and family.

He looks at Mom now and asks, “How long was I under?”

“Three days and nights,” she replies, shaking her head wistfully while stroking hair back from his forehead.

He thinks a little, looking into the luminous box of light over the bed. He grins.

“Happy Easter,” he says.

White Elephants

We have all come back this Christmas to the acreage shared by my parents and Nat's family: all three sons and wives and six grown children. We are sleeping at both houses, but we gather at Nat's place to save Mom and Dad the strain of serving food. We have decided to share "white elephant" gifts so that we won't stress them about gifts either. And partway through the opening of this grab bag of oddities, our son Luke pulls out a zebra-print loin cloth that my brother Nat manufactured in his basement shop using a pair of Lycra "Under Armour," some throwaway fabric, and a bunch of metal grommets.

When eighteen-year-old Luke, the youngest of the kids, comes out of the bathroom, bare-skinned except for this Under Armour and a ridiculous flap of striped black and white cloth, everyone hoots and hollers and whistles, and suddenly to our mutual surprise there is a tangle of yellow filament arcing everywhere. Apparently my father, hunched on the couch under a blanket, has decided to use his own white elephant gift—a spray can of Silly String.

Luke ducks and sidesteps but to no avail. Soon he is covered with coils of the foamy string. And everyone is laughing uproariously, delighted that Dad, despite his feebleness, is still able to surprise. We laugh all the harder because this is not an easy time for us to find pleasure. I am conscious—we are *all* conscious—of the gap in the house which used to be filled by nephew Alex. To see Luke prancing in his zebra-skin loincloth is bittersweet because he is the exact age that Alex would be. He has the same lanky look—no doubt reminding Nat and Marcia of their loss. And though he is clearly happy, I know just how much Luke was wrenched by the disappearance of that "other brother." I remember him weeping with his head down on our kitchen island, shoulders heaving. When we tried to console him, saying we were sorry that he should have to experience such a loss, he finally said, in a cracked muffled voice, "I thought we were going to get old together and share it all."

Who knew that my eighty-four--year-old father would outlive my seventeen-year-old nephew? And who knew, given Dad's massive heart attack, that he would still be here for yet another Christmas?

Back from his near-death experience, my father seems himself but not himself. Gaunt, sagging from his bones, he gets chilled easily. There is no more cutting brush or walking the road, not with his heart reduced to 40% of its output. Instead, he has to sit and exercise his lungs, blowing into a clear plastic tube to make a ping pong ball rise. When I call to check in on him, he lapses into silence, letting my mother carry the conversation. He is retreating slowly, turning over the control. He lives by proxy, and I know what is being signaled. A couple weeks? A few months? The days are numbered.

Suddenly, I think back to when I was only twelve and Dad lost his own father, Doc K.F., with his bushy eyebrows and steady hands. I am reminded of Grandma Lillian too, who used to say, "The wind is *always* blowing, but *you* have to raise the sail." When Grandma passed away at eighty-seven, Dad admitted to me that he felt unprotected—as if he had lost the last barrier between him and his own death. I look at him now—sitting on Nat's couch, shrunken under his furry brown blanket—and I understand just what he meant. I feel the impending threat, the crumbling of the fortress walls that have kept me safe all these years.

My wife pulls out her own white elephant gift, which turns out to be a pair of plastic teeth that are horribly disfigured—big slanted buckteeth, brown with imitation decay. When she pops them into her mouth and grins, the clan breaks into another gale of laughter.

Everyone is roaring and wiping at their eyes—even my decrepit dad. I kneel forward with my cellphone, down on one knee like a supplicant, and I snap three or four quick photos. He coughs as he guffaws, thumping his chest, but his eyes glitter. He shoots more Silly String into the air.

As it turns out, these will be the last photos I take of Dad. The next time I see him he will be in the hospital, barely conscious, about to be transferred to hospice. And then there will only be a few days of disjointed conversation.

Climbing Lesson 6

"Hey Dad, sorry to wake you. Just wanted to check in. How's it going?"

"Still dying."

"C'mon, you know what I mean."

"You mean okay with dying?"

"I don't know. You tell me."

"Negative."

"We can talk sports, instead."

"Once asked Dad that question."

"What question?"

"What it's like to be dying."

"That's not what I asked."

"Well, it's what you're wondering…"

"I'm just wondering how you're doing, Dad. That's all. And I'm starting to think they've got you on too many pain killers."

"Telling you, been there. Sitting in the guest chair with my own father."

"Okay, then. What was that like? When you asked Grandpa about dying, what did he say?"

"Some things public, some private."

"Point taken. Does that still stand?"

"Just know I needed to talk—like you. Got double vision now. Can see both ways."

"Is that good?"

"Strange. Like being stuck in a doorway."

"Hey, you look like something's hurting. Is it your throat again? Maybe you should rest..."

"No. That was him. This is me."

"Good. Because I'm glad you are who you are—glad you're my dad."

"That's what I wanted to say."

"When? To your dad?"

"Some things public, some private."

"You mean he wouldn't let you share what you felt?"

"Don't know, maybe he heard. Where's the nurse? I push the button, but no one comes."

"That bad, eh?"

"Worse."

"Sure it's not you? You know, doctors make the worst patients."

"Except for nurses. These ones should have worked at a morgue."

"So we're done talking about dying?"

"Done for now. Which is okay. You can tell 'em IV needs changing. I'm going t'sleep. Be in a better mood.

Still older than you."

"Good to hear. Then I'll stay younger. I'll come over in my usual role, and you can play your role. Let's keep it that way."

"For a day or two. I can manage. But you'll get your turn. Trust me, we all do."

Postscript: A Few Reading Tips

If you would like to reflect about the stories in *Climbing Lessons*, either alone or in a group, here are three strategies I recommend:

1. Pick a story that resonates with you and consider why you connect to it. How are you like one of the characters, either in personality or role? How are you different? Also, what emotion is being awakened in you—such as sadness, joy, humor, or anger—and why do you think you are being impacted that way?

2. Turn a sheet of paper sideways and create a timeline of your relationship to your father or son. Above the line, write the relevant dates and events. Below the line, write notes about what you felt at the time and what you were/are discovering. What parallels

do you see between your experiences and the stories in *Climbing Lessons*?

3. Think of all these inter-linked stories as a display case illustrating the stages of human development. Then consider how well the characters deal with the main challenges of those stages.

Psychologist Erik Erickson defined eight basic stages, and he claimed that humans wrestle with distinct "crises" during each period of this progression. You can learn more about his stages online, but here is a quick overview.

Stage One (0-1 ½ years): As infants, we wrestle with whether to trust the world around us. If our parents make us feel safe, we learn trust, which leads to hopefulness instead of anxiety.

Stages Two (1 ½ -3) and Three (3-5): As we move into toddlerhood, we learn autonomy, experimenting with our own latent initiative. Willfulness and productivity are good by-products, as opposed to shame or guilt.

Stage Four (5-12): According to Erickson's model, when we hit the grade school years, we need to discover our industriousness, learning a new level of competence, or we will struggle with inferiority.

Stage Five (12-18): Adolescence is one of the hardest stages because we are trying to forge a reliable sense of self. Finding one's identity requires trying options, which can be confusing. The successful adolescent starts to claim his or her own gifts and temperament. He or she arrives at what Erickson calls "fidelity."

Stage Six (18-40): Intimacy vs. isolation is the crisis of early adulthood. We need to step away from parents, forming our own family or community. Otherwise, we will feel alone and unworthy.

Stage Seven (40-65): Generativity vs. stagnation—that is the central crisis of the middle years of adulthood, when we try to reach our full potential, providing for others as well as the self.

Stage Eight (65+): When old age arrives, we hope to experience integrity rather than despair, looking back with wisdom instead of feeling fooled.

If you take time to apply Erickson's model of human development to these stories, you will find that, like a multi-faceted lens or prism, it will reveal an array of hidden colors. For instance, if you apply Erickson's model to the frail grandfather lying in the hospital and remembering his father's death, then you are likely to ask this important question: "Is he finding integrity at this late stage, or despair?"

Or take Erickson's "lens" to the younger father, and ask why he is choked up while watching his grade school son execute a fake reverse in flag football? Has he been feeling generative at this point in his life, or stagnant? Did something change, and why?

Or look at the grade school boy who feels so happy when his father helps him dig a cave. What would

Erickson say is happening in terms of the boy's sense of initiative or industry?

Whatever stage of life you are considering, just think about the archetypal "crisis" that Erickson assigns. Then reflect on how well the relevant character is dealing with that challenge.

And here comes the fun part! When you have practiced a bit, take the same developmental model to your own set of life stories. Were some stages easier or harder for you, as you matured? Why? And what about your father or your child? What stages might have been especially easy or hard for them? Finally, how might these past experiences be shaping the way you interact with your father or child?

Erickson's research demonstrated that any developmental "crisis" that was not resolved in its standard time period would continue to demand attention later. He discovered, however, that people could reach a delayed resolution, depending on their relationships and their life-choices. So what do you now see about your relationship to your father or your child, and how might that relationship improve? Over time, every relationship must change, but don't forget that it can change for the better.

Acknowledgments

This book began a long time ago, with two essays that appeared in print: "Cold Storage," published in the summer 2011 issue of *Thema*, and "Floating," published in the fall 2011 issue of *Natural Bridge*. However, *Climbing Lessons* would not have become a full book without the dream-come-true of a one-month writing residency at the Anderson Arts Center in Redwing, Minnesota. A big thank you to the staff there, in particular Chris Burawa and Shawn Niebeling. I also want to acknowledge my editor, Elizabeth Turnbull, who believed in *Climbing Lessons* and provided excellent advice, working with the remarkable staff at Light Messages to make the book look snazzy and to get it out there into the world! Finally, thanks to my sons Conrad and Luke, who have read and responded generously, allowing me to tell my version of our shared story. And thanks to my ever-wise wife, Cathleen, who has been a superb behind-the-scenes editor for nearly 35 years.

The Author

Tim Bascom is the author of five books, including the memoirs *Chameleon Days* (winner of the Bakeless Prize in Nonfiction) and *Running to the Fire* (Finalist for the Indiefab Memoir of the Year). The memoirs chronicle years spent in Ethiopia, where his father served as a medical missionary before and during the revolution that overthrew Emperor Haile Selassie. Tim's essays have been published in major anthologies such as *Best Creative Nonfiction* and *Best American Travel Writing*. As a native Kansan, he has lived most of his life in the prairie region of the U.S. In *Climbing Lessons*, he draws on the experience of four generations of his Midwestern family. Sometimes, when schedules allow, he still plays soccer with his grown sons, who love to debate with him.

Tim is available for readings and interviews, and can be reached at timbascom.wordpress.com.

You Might Also Like

In the financial district of Des Moines, Iowa, stands a historic Episcopal cathedral connected to several acres of restored prairie. When hotel developers approach Brigid Brenchley, the kind and quirky cathedral dean, she and her parishioners much choose between their passion for the prairie restoration and their need for money to repair the crumbling cathedral. Of course, the parish's largest donor stands to profit from the deal. The creation? Or the cash? As flood waters rise, so do the stakes of their choice.

You Might Also Like

In his latest collection of essays and poems Taylor-Troutman guides readers through seemingly simple stories of death, life, parenting struggles, successes and failures that speak to larger questions we all face: How do we best spend our time? How can we raise our kids to be kind and confident? Who gives us guidance and wisdom? What does love look like in our lives on a day-to-day basis? In simple and important gestures like cleaning spilled milk with toilet paper, flipping the perfect pancake with your partner, and walking down the beach with your young child, readers find universal truths to guide their own lives regardless of personal circumstances.